Hinduism is a living organism
liable to growth and decay,
subject to laws of Nature...
the changes in seasons affect it.
It has autumn and its summer,
its winter and spring. It is, and
it is not, based on scriptures.
It does not derive its authority
from one book.

— *Gandhi*

Acclaim

Swami Vivekananda

Hindu religion does not consist in struggles and in attempts to believe a certain doctrine or a dogma, but in realizing, in being and becoming.

Annie Besant

After a study of some forty years of the great religions of the world, I find none so scientific, none so philosophical and none so spiritual than Hinduism.

S. Radhakrishnan

Hinduism is a unified mass of spiritual thought and realization. ...(it) is an inheritance of thought and aspiration, living and moving with the movement of life itself.

Sir V. S. Naipaul

To speak of Hindu fundamentalism, is a contradiction in terms, it does not exist. Hinduism is not this kind of religion.

Hermann Keyserling
German Philosopher

Hinduism has spoken only the relevant truth about the way to self-realisation.

Sri Aurobindo

That which we call the Hindu religion is really the Eternal religion because it embraces all others... it is a continously enlarging tradition of the Godward endeavour of the human spirit.

Hinduism

According to **Gandhi**

Thoughts, Writings

and

Critical Interpretation

Orient Publishing

DELHI | MUMBAI | HYDERABAD

This is the revised and enlarged edition of *Hindu Dharma* first published in association with the Navajivan Trust in Orient Paperbacks in 1978 and reprinted several times.

ISBN : 978-81-222-0558-9

Hinduism: According to Gandhi

Subject: Religion / Hinduism

1st Published 2013
2nd Printing 2014

Published by
Orient Publishing
(an imprint of Orient Paperbacks)
5A/8 Ansari Road, Darya Ganj, New Delhi-110 002
www.orientpublishing.com

Printed at
Saurabh Printers Pvt. Ltd., Noida, India

Cover Printed at
Ravindra Printing Press, Delhi-110 006, India

To the Reader

I would like to say to the diligent reader of my writings and to others who are interested in them that I am not at all concerned with appearing to be consistent. In my search after Truth I have discarded many ideas and learnt many new things.

What I am concerned with is my readiness to obey the call of Truth, my God, from moment to moment, and therefore when anybody finds any inconsistency between any two writings of mine, if he has still faith in my sanity, he would do well to choose the later of the two on the same subject.

M.K. Gandhi

Harijan, April 29, 1933

Publisher's Note

Hinduism was not founded by any individual; it has evolved naturally and therefore remains gloriously undefined. At best Hinduism is a working hypothesis of human conduct adapted to different stages of spiritual development and different conditions of life.

In the words of Dr S Radhakrishnan, 'It is more a way of life than a form of thought... The theist and the atheist, the skeptic and the agnostic may all be Hindus if they accept the Hindu system of culture and life. Hinduism insists not on religious conformity but on a spiritual and ethical outlook of life...'

Gandhi was not a scholar of Hindu religion, and did not consider himself fit to interpret Hinduism except through his own experience. He applied his own intellect and reason to the Hindu way of life. In the Jan. 12, 1934 issue of *Harijan* he wrote, '...I have no hesitation in putting before the public, with utmost confidence, the conclusions I have reached regarding certain fundamentals of Hinduism.'

This book is thoughtful selection of Gandhi's writings, thoughts and public discourses on Hinduism. Many of his expressions were spontaneous and unrehearsed. In an effort to retain the essence of his thinking and make it more readable, the original text has been respectfully abridged at a few places. However every effort has been made to be as close to the original meaning as is possible.

Contents

To the Reader

Publisher's Note

1. Why I am a Hindu / 11

2. Different Aspects of Hinduism / 14

3. Hinduism: A Living Organism / 20

4. Who is a Hindu? / 23

5. The Spirit of Hinduism / 25

6. Evolution of the Hindus / 33

7. How may Scriptures be Interpreted / 39

8. Who is a *Sanatani* Hindu? / 43

9. *Varnashrama:* A Critical Interpretation / 48

10. What has Hinduism Done for Us? / 52

11. No Contradiction between the Jain and the Vedic Doctrine / 56

12. The True Meaning of *Yajna* / 61

13. Importance of *Tapas* / 66

14. *Brahmacharya:* Search for the *Brahman* / 68

15. The Nature of *Atman* / 73

16. God is All Things to All Men / 75
17. Belief in God: One Yet Many / 77
18. God: The Indefinable Power / 81
19. *Advaitism* and God / 85
20. Never Lose Faith in God / 88
21. Equality of Religions / 90
22. The Traditions of Self Purification / 95
23. Power of *Ramanama* / 98
24. *Ramanama:* One of the Many Names of God / 107
25. Significance of *Dwija* Ceremony / 109
26. Tulsidas and *Ramayana* / 111
27. *Bhaktiyoga:* Realisation of God through Devotion / 115
28. *Anasaktiyoga:* The Gospel of Selfless Action / 118
29. Are *Shastras* Infallible? / 127
30. *Manusmriti* / 129
31. Significance of Shri Krishna's Life / 130
32. How to Celebrate Diwali? / 133
33. Who is a True *Vaishnava?* / 136
34. The Chief Value of Hinduism / 139
35. Hindu Code of Conduct / 141
36. Is there Satan in Hinduism? / 147

Glossary
Bibliography

Hinduism is like the Ganges,
pure and unsullied at its source,
but taking in its course the impurities
in the way. Even like the Ganges
it is beneficent in its
total effect. It takes
a provincial form
in every province,
but the inner
substance is
retained everywhere.

Hinduism
has proven much more open than any other religion to new ideas, scientific thought, and social experimentation.

It would not be surprising to find Hinduism the dominant religion of the twenty-first century.

It would be a religion that doctrinally is less clear-cut than mainstream Christianity, politically less determined than Islam, ethically less heroic than Buddhism, but it would offer something to everybody.

It will appear idealistic to those who look for idealism, pragmatic to the pragmatists, spiritual to the seekers, sensual to the here-and-now generation.

Klaus L. Klostermaier
Professor of Religious Studies at the University of Manitoba,
and former Director of Academic Affairs,
Oxford Centre for Hindu Studies

1

Why I am a Hindu

An American friend who subscribes herself as a lifelong friend of India writes:

> As Hinduism is one of the prominent religions of the East, and as you have made a study of Christianity and Hinduism, and on the basis of that study have announced that you are a Hindu, I beg leave to ask of you if you will do me the favour to give me your reasons for that choice. Hindus and Christians alike realize that man's chief need is to know God and to worship Him in spirit and in truth. Believing that Christ was a revelation of God, Christians of America have sent to India thousands of their sons and daughters to tell the people of India about Christ. Will you in return kindly give us your interpretation of Hinduism and make a comparison of Hinduism with the teachings of Christ? I will be deeply grateful for this favour.

I have ventured at several missionary meetings to tell English and American missionaries that if they could have refrained from 'telling' India about Christ and had merely lived the life enjoined upon them by the 'Sermon on the Mount', India instead of suspecting them would have appreciated their living in the midst of her children and directly profited by their presence. Holding this view, I can 'tell' American friends nothing about Hinduism by way of 'return'. I do not believe in people telling others of their faith, especially with a view to conversion. Faith does not admit of telling. It has to be lived and then it becomes self-propagating.

Nor do I consider myself fit to interpret Hinduism except through my own life. And if I may not interpret Hinduism through my written word, I may not compare it with Christianity. The only thing possible for me therefore to do, is to say, as briefly as I can, why I am a Hindu.

Believing as I do in the influence of heredity, being born in a Hindu family, I have remained a Hindu. I should reject it, if I found it inconsistent with my moral sense or my spiritual growth. On examination, I have found it to be the most tolerant of all religions known to me. Its freedom from dogma makes a forcible appeal to me inasmuch as it gives the votary the largest scope for self-expression. Not being an exclusive religion, it enables the followers of that faith not merely to respect all the other religions, but it also enables them to admire and assimilate whatever may be good in the other faiths.

Non-violence is common to all religions, but it has found the highest expression and application in Hinduism. (I do not regard Jainism or Buddhism as separate from Hinduism). Hinduism believes in the oneness not of merely all human life but in the oneness of all that lives. Its worship of the cow is, in my opinion, its unique contribution to the evolution of humanitarianism. It is a practical application of the belief in the oneness and, therefore, sacredness of all life. The great belief in transmigration is a direct consequence of that belief.

Finally the discovery of the law of *varnashrama* is a magnificent result of the ceaseless search for truth. I hope to have to say more on *varnashrama* in the near future. In this all-too-brief a sketch I have mentioned what occur to me to be the outstanding features of Hinduism that keep me in its fold.

2

Different Aspects of Hinduism[1]

I have asserted my claim to being a *sanatani* Hindu with greater emphasis than hitherto, and yet there are things which are commonly done in the name of Hinduism, which I disregard. I have no desire to be called a *sanatani* Hindu or any other if I am not such. And I have certainly no desire to steal in a reform or an abuse under cover of a great faith.

It is therefore necessary for me once and for all distinctly to give my meaning of *sanatana* Hinduism. The word *sanatana* I use in its natural sense.

I call myself a *sanatani* Hindu, because,

1. I believe in the Vedas, the Upanishads, the Puranas and all that goes by the name of Hindu scriptures, and therefore in *avatars* and rebirth,
2. I believe in the *varnashrama dharma* in a sense in my opinion strictly Vedic, but not in its present popular and crude sense,

[1] Originally published under the title *Aspects of Hinduism* in *Young India.*

3. I believe in the protection of the cow in its much larger sense than the popular, and

4. I do not disbelieve in idol-worship.

The reader will note that I have purposely refrained from using the word divine origin in reference to the Vedas or any other scriptures. For I do not believe in the exclusive divinity of the Vedas. I believe the Bible, the Koran, and the Zend-Avesta[2] to be as much divinely inspired as the Vedas.

My belief in the Hindu scriptures does not require me to accept every word and every verse as divinely inspired. Nor do I claim to have any first-hand knowledge of these wonderful books. But I do claim to know and feel the truths of the essential teaching of the scriptures.

I decline to be bound by any interpretation, however learned it may be, if it is repugnant to reason or moral sense. I do most emphatically repudiate the claim (if they advance any such) of the present Shankaracharyas[3] and *shastris* to give a correct interpretation of the Hindu scriptures.

On the contrary I believe that our present knowledge of these books is in a most chaotic state. I believe implicitly in the Hindu aphorism, that no one truly knows the Shastras who has not attained perfection in innocence *(ahimsa),* truth *(satya)* and self-control *(brahmacharya),* and who has not renounced all acquisition or possession of wealth.

I believe in the institution of gurus, but in this age millions must go without a guru, because it is a rare thing to find a combination of perfect purity and perfect learning. But one need not despair of ever knowing the truth of one's religion,

---

[2] The Zoroastrian sacred writings, comprising the Avesta (the text) and Zend (the commentary).

[3] 780-812; Hindu philosopher and religious reformer; author of commentaries.

because the fundamentals of Hinduism as of every great religion are unchangeable, and easily understood.

Every Hindu believes in God and His oneness, in rebirth and salvation. But that which distinguishes Hinduism from every other religion is its cow-protection, more than its *varnashrama.*

~

Varnashrama is, in my opinion, inherent in human nature, and Hinduism has simply reduced it to a science. It does attach to birth. A man cannot change his *varna* by choice. Not to abide by one's *varna* is to disregard the law of heredity. The division, however, into innumerable castes is an unwarranted liberty taken with the doctrine. The four divisions are all-sufficing.

I do not believe that inter-dining or even inter-marriage necessarily deprives a man of his status that his birth has given him. The four divisions define a man's calling, they do not restrict or regulate social intercourse. The divisions define duties, they confer no privileges. It is, I hold, against the genius of Hinduism to arrogate to oneself a higher status or assign to another a lower. All are born to serve God's creation, a Brahmin with his knowledge, a Kshatriya with his power of protection, a Vaisya with his commercial ability and a Sudra with his bodily labour.

This however does not mean that a Brahmin for instance is absolved from bodily labour, or the duty of protecting himself and others. His birth makes a Brahmin predominantly a man of knowledge, the fittest by heredity and training to impart it to others. There is nothing, again, to prevent the Sudra from acquiring all the knowledge he wishes. Only, he will best serve with his body and need not envy others their special qualities for service. But a Brahmin who claims superiority by right of knowledge falls, and has no knowledge. And so with the others who pride themselves upon their special qualities. *Varnashrama* is self-restraint and conservation and economy of energy.

Though therefore *varnashrama* is not affected by inter-dining or inter-marriage, Hinduism does most emphatically discourage inter-dining and inter-marriage between divisions.

~

Hinduism reached the highest limit of self-restraint. It is undoubtedly a religion of renunciation of the flesh so that the spirit may be set free.

Salvation is freedom from birth and hence death also. Prohibition against inter-marriage and inter-dining is essential for a rapid evolution of the soul. But this self-denial is no test of *varna.* A Brahmin may remain a Brahmin, though he may dine with his Sudra brother, if he has not left off his duty of service by knowledge. It follows from what I have said above, that restraint in matters of marriage and dining is not based upon notions of superiority. A Hindu who refuses to dine with another from a sense of superiority misrepresents his *dharma.*

~

The central fact of Hinduism however is cow-protection. Cow protection to me is one of the most wonderful phenomena in human evolution. It takes the human being beyond his species. The cow is enjoined to realize his identity with all that lives. Why the cow was selected for apotheosis is obvious to me. The cow was in India the best companion. She was the giver of plenty. Not only did she give milk, but she also made agriculture possible. She is the mother to millions of Indian mankind. Protection of the cow means protection of the whole dumb creation of God.

The way to protect is to die for her. It is a denial of Hinduism and *ahimsa* to kill a human being to protect a cow. Hindus are enjoined to protect the cow by their *tapasya*, by self-purification, by self-sacrifice.

By every act of cruelty to our cattle, we disown God and Hinduism. I do not know that the condition of the cattle in any other part of the world is so bad as in unhappy India. We may plead poverty in our defence. Criminal negligence is the only cause of the miserable condition of our cattle. Our *pinjrapoles*, though they are an answer to our instinct of mercy, are a clumsy demonstration of its execution. Instead of being model dairy farms and great profitable national institutions, they are merely depots for receiving decrepit cattle.

Hindus will be judged not by their *tilaks,* not by the correct chanting of *mantras,* not by their pilgrimages, not by their most punctilious observance of caste rules but by their ability to protect the cow. Whilst professing the religion of cow-protection, we have enslaved the cow and her progeny, and have become slaves ourselves.

~

I can no more describe my feeling for Hinduism than for my own wife. She moves me as no other woman in the world can. Not that she has no faults. I dare say she has many more than I see myself. But the feeling of an indissoluble bond is there. Even so I feel for and about Hinduism with all its faults and limitations. Nothing elates me so much as the music of the *Gita* or the *Ramayana* by Tulsidas, the only two books in Hinduism I may be said to know. When I fancied I was taking my last breath, the *Gita* was my solace.

I know the vice that is going on today in all the great Hindu shrines, but I love them in spite of their unspeakable failings.

There is an interest which I take in them and which I take in no other. I am a reformer through and through. But my zeal never takes me to the rejection of any of the essential things of Hinduism. I have said I do not disbelieve in idol-worship. An idol does not excite any feeling of veneration in me. But I think that idol-worship is part of human nature. We hanker after symbolism. Why should one be more composed in a church than elsewhere? Images are an aid to worship. No Hindu considers an image to be God. I do not consider idol-worship a sin.

It is clear from the foregoing, that Hinduism is not an exclusive religion. In it there is room for the worship of all the prophets of the world. It is not a missionary religion in the ordinary sense of the term. It has no doubt absorbed many tribes in its fold, but this absorption has been of an evolutionary imperceptible character. Hinduism tells everyone to worship God according to his own faith or *dharma,* and so it lives at peace with all the religions.

Hinduism is a growth of ages. The very name, Hinduism, was given to the religion of the people of Hindustan by foreigners.

3

Hinduism: A Living Organism[1]

Hinduism is a living organism liable to growth and decay, and subject to the laws of Nature. One, and indivisible at the root, it has grown into a vast tree with innumerable branches. The changes in the seasons affect it. It has its autumn and summer, its winter and spring. The rains nourish and fructify it too. It is and is not based on scriptures. It does not derive its authority from one book. The *Gita* is universally accepted, but even then it only shows the way. It has hardly any effect on custom. Hinduism is like the Ganges, pure and unsullied at its source, but taking in its course the impurities in the way. Even like the Ganges it is beneficent in its total effect. It takes a provincial form in every province, but the inner substance is retained everywhere. Custom is not religion. Custom may change, but religion will remain unaltered.

Purity of Hinduism depends on the self-restraint of its votaries. Whenever their religion has been in danger, the Hindus

[1] The Gujarati original of this appeared in *Navajivan,* February 7, 1926. This is a translation by Mahadev Desai which was originally published under the title *Hinduism of Today* in *Young India.*

have undergone rigorous penance, searched the causes of the danger and devised means for combating them. The Shastras are ever-growing. The Vedas, Upanishads, Smritis, Puranas and Itihasas did not arise at one and the same time. Each grew out of the necessities of particular periods, and therefore they seem to conflict with one another. These books do not enunciate anew the eternal truths but show how these were practised at the time to which the books belong.

A practice which was good enough in a particular period would, if blindly repeated in another, land people into the 'slough of despond'. Because the practice of animal-sacrifice obtained at one time, shall we revive it today? Because at one time, we used to eat beef, shall we revive it today? Because at one time, we used to chop off the hands and the feet of thieves, shall we revive that barbarity today? Shall we revive polyandry? Shall we revive child-marriages? Because we discarded a section of humanity one day, shall we brand their descendants today as outcastes?

Hinduism abhors stagnation. Knowledge is limitless and so also the application of truth. Everyday we add to our knowledge the power of *atman,* and we shall keep on doing so. New experience will teach us new duties, but truth shall ever be the same.

Who has ever known it in its entirety? The Vedas represent the truth, they are infinite. But who has known them in their entirety? What has ever been known in its entirety? What goes today by the name of the Vedas are not even a millionth part of the real Veda — the *Book of Knowledge*. And who knows the entire meaning of even the few books that we have?

Rather than wade through these infinite complications, our sages taught us to learn one thing: 'As with the self, so with the Universe.' It is not possible to scan the universe, as it is to scan the self. Know the self and you know the universe. But even knowledge of the self within presupposes ceaseless striving — not only ceaseless but pure, and pure striving presupposes a pure heart, which in its turn depends on the practice of *yamas* and *niyamas* — the cardinal and causal virtues.

This practice is not possible without God's grace which presupposes faith and devotion. This is why Tulsidas sang of the glory of *Ramanama,* that is why the author of the *Bhagavata* taught the *dwadashamantra.* To my mind he is a *sanatani* Hindu who can repeat this mantra from the heart. All else is a bottomless pit, as the sage Akho[2] has said.

Boycott of beef-eaters may have been proper in the past. It is improper and impossible today. Non-violent efforts to wean them away from their bad habits are going on, but Hinduism does not consist in eating and not eating. Its kernel consists in right conduct, in correct observance of truth and non-violence. Many a man eating meat, but observing the cardinal virtues of compassion and truth, and living in the fear of God, is a better Hindu than a hypocrite who abstains from meat. And he whose eyes are opened to the truth of the violence in beef-eating or meat-eating and who has therefore rejected them, who loves 'both man and bird and beast' is worthy of our adoration. He has seen and known God: he is His best devotee. He is the teacher of mankind.

Hinduism and all other religions are being weighed in the balance. Eternal truth is one. God is one. Let everyone of us steer clear of conflicting creeds and customs and follow the straight path of truth. Only then shall we be true Hindus. Many styling themselves *sanatanis* stalk the earth. Who knows how few of them will be chosen by God! God's grace shall descend on those who do His will and wait upon Him, not on those who simply mutter 'Ram Ram'.

---

[2] A poet seer of Gujarat.

4

Who Is a Hindu?

Correspondence of Gandhiji which appeared under the title 'Correspondence: A Cathechism' in which he responded to the question posed by the writer of the letter.

Question: You have always termed yourself a 'Hindu'. On the other hand you are not ready to accept the dictates of the Hindu pandits or even their Shastras concerning child-marriage, widow-remarriage, untouchability, etc. You say in *Young India* dated August 26: 'The *Smritis* bristle with contradictions. Inspiring verses on self-restraint could not be written at the same time and by the same pen that wrote the verses encouraging the brute in man.' The same, I submit, might be said of the many *Puranas* of the Hindus. Denying the authority of these books, I do not understand how you can call yourself a 'Hindu' (as understood at present) who has an implicit faith in the absurdities and immoralities (derogatory to common sense) preached by some of the *Puranas*. If you think it is not necessary for a Hindu to believe so, it would be in the service of truth if you were to define the Hindu religion and clear the arguments for your being regarded a Hindu.

You would not say a man is a 'Hindu', if he likes to call himself a Hindu, even though he does not follow the doctrine and Shastric injunction of the latter. Thus if I were to term myself a Christian and say that it is not necessary for a true Christian to have faith in the Bible or even Christ, I could only be termed a pretender.

Besides when you disagree in the matter of *Shastras* from the Hindus, it requires to be explained why you should prefer to call yourself a Hindu (in spite of the evil associations connected with this word and in spite of the word not being found in any *Shastra* of the Hindus even) and not an 'Arya' which is a better term even in itself. Besides your teachings as regards the interpretation of the Hindu Shastras have much in common with those of Arya Samaj.

Gandhi's reply: I call myself Sanatani Hindu, because I believe in the *Vedas, Upanishads,* the *Puranas* and the writings left by the holy reformers. This belief does not require me to accept as authentic everything that passes as *Shastras.* I reject everything that contradicts the fundamental principles of morality. I am not required to accept the *ipse dixit* or the interpretations of pundits.

Above all I call myself a Sanatani Hindu, so long as the Hindu society in general accepts me as such. In a concrete manner he is a Hindu who believes in God, immortality of the soul, transmigration, the law of karma and moksha, and who tries to practice truth and ahimsa in daily life, and therefore practices cow-protection in its widest sense and understands and tries to act according to the law of Varnashrama.

5

The Spirit of Hinduism[1]

Mr. M.K. Gandhi delivered the first of a series of lectures on Hinduism in Johannesburg on March 04, 1905 at the Masonic Temple, Plane Street, Johannesburg, under the auspices of the Johannesburg Lodge of the Theosophical Society. Major Peacock, vice-president, was in the chair.

Mr. Gandhi introduced his subject by remarking that the endeavours of the Johannesburg Lodge to promote interest in the study of different religious systems were most praiseworthy, tending as they did, to widen people's sympathies, and enlarge their comprehension of the motives and beliefs underlying the actions of those who were strangers in creed and colour. He himself had endeavoured, during his eleven years' residence in South Africa, to remove the prejudice and ignorance that existed concerning his own people.

Continuing, the lecturer described what was meant by the title 'Hindu', referring it to the branch of the Aryan people

1 Originally published under the title *Two Lectures on Hinduism* in *Collected Works of M K Gandhi, Vol 4, May 4, 1904-Nov 4, 1905.*

that had migrated to the trans-Indus-districts of India, and had colonised that vast country. As a matter of fact, Aryanism would have been a better descriptive word than Hinduism, in explanation of the faith accepted by so many millions of his countrymen.

One of the most remarkable characteristics of the religion professed by Hindus was self-abnegation, and this was obviously shown in the name of the religion itself, for, unlike most of the great world religions, it did not derive its name from any prophet or teacher, although it counted some of the greatest within its fold. The lecturer further instanced the historic siege of Arcot in support of this contention, when the Indian soldiers, at a time when starvation faced the whole British Army, waived their claim to the rice rations in favour of the British soldiers, they themselves being content to have the water in which the rice had been boiled, although it was customary to throw this water away; and also the case of Prabhu Singh, an indentured British Indian, (vide letter to Dadabhai Naoroji[2] October 08, 1900 and *satyagrah* in South Africa, Chap IX) who was chosen for the post of honour of warning the inhabitants of Lady-Smith during the siege, whenever a Boer shell was coming, by ringing a bell while perched in a tree, at imminent risk to himself. This man was mentioned several times in despatches by Sir George White[3].

~

The Hindus themselves claimed that the date of their scriptures was veiled in the mist of antiquity, the scriptures themselves being God-given. As against that, some Europeans contended that the scriptures were not more than 3,000 or 4,000 years

---

[2] Known as 'Father of Indian nationalism' and the first Indian to ask for Self-government.

[3] Lieutenant General, Commander of English Forces in South Africa.

Hinduism
is not an exclusive religion.
In it there is room for the worship
of all the prophets of the world.
It is not a missionary religion
in the ordinary sense of the term.
It has no doubt absorbed many tribes
in its fold, but this absorption
has been of an evolutionary
imperceptible character.

old. Mr. Tilak[4] a well-known Indian Sanskritist, has, however, calculated that, from certain astronomical observations made in these works, they were at least 10,000 years old, although they were only committed to writing some three hundred years after Christ. The Vedas, as these scriptures were known, consisted of separate hymns, each being held to cover a definite period, and quite independent of each other. And, typically, not one author's name had passed down to posterity. The Vedas had inspired the thought of many illustrious men of the West, amongst whom might be mentioned Arthur Schopenhauer[5] and Professor Max Muller[6].

Over two hundred millions of people professed Hinduism, and this faith entered into their every act. The key-note of Hinduism on the spiritual side was *moksha,* or salvation; that is, the final absorption of the Soul in the Infinite Soul that pervades all things.

In regard to religion, pantheism was the chief characteristic, whilst, on the ethical plane, self-abnegation was the most notable quality, with its corollary, toleration. In social matters, the characteristic of caste was predominant, whilst the ceremonial characteristic was the sacrificing of animals. At a time when the faith of the Hindus had become more formal, Prince Gautama Buddha having learnt the spiritual worth of things during a prolonged period of contemplation, commenced to teach that animal sacrifices were despiritualising, and that the highest

[4] Bal Gangadhar Tilak.

[5] 19th century German philosopher who was deeply influenced by Eastern thought and Vedantic tradition.

[6] German philologist scholar and orientalist best known for his study of Indology and comparative religions.

form of love was expressed by extending that toleration, which was already a tenet of their faith, in the direction of refraining from killing or otherwise destroying living things.

Hinduism had never, as a religion, been missionary, as were Christianity and Mahomedanism, but, under King Asoka, the Buddhist priests were sent far and wide to propagate the new belief. Buddhism had a reforming effect upon Hinduism, somewhat similar to that of Protestantism upon Catholicism, but there was a great difference in the spirit underlying that reform. No Hindu bore the Buddhist any ill-will, a statement that could not be made in reference to the Protestants and Catholics. Buddhism was sometimes said to have declined in India. This was not really so. The Buddhist priests had endeavoured to propagate their faith too zealously, and had aroused the jealousy, at the time of the Hindu priesthood, who had driven the Buddhists to the outskirts of the country, to Tibet, China, Japan, Burma (now Myanmar) and Ceylon (now Sri Lanka). But the spirit of the Buddhists remained in India, and actuated every principle professed by the Hindus.

~

In this connection, the lecturer briefly referred to Jainism as a most interesting form of faith. The Jains claimed that it was altogether independent of Buddhism, not a growth from it. Unlike others, they did not claim for the faith that it was of divine origin, recognising that its sacred writings were the results of human workmanship. Jainism was, perhaps the most logical of faiths, and its most remarkable characteristic was its scrupulous regard for all things that lived.

Spirit of Hinduism: 2nd Lecture

Gandhi delivered his second lecture on 'Hinduism' under the auspices of Johannesburg Theosophical Lodge, at the Masonic Temple on March 11, 1905.

The lecturer, after giving a short resume of the previous lecture, said that the second lecture would be devoted to what might be termed the second epoch of Hinduism.

After the reformation that took place from within, under the influence of the teachings of Buddha, Hinduism was very largely addicted to idolatry. Several explanations were offered in extenuation, but the lecturer could not deny the fact that the Hindus seemingly worshipped stocks and stones. The Hindu philosophers easily recognised and worshipped God as the purest spirit, and pantheism took them to the highest flight. It similarly, brought down the ignorant masses to the lowest depths. If the infant mind could not realise God as a pure spirit, it had no difficulty in worshipping Him through His various manifestations. Many worship Him through the sun, the moon and the stars, and many worship Him through stocks and stones also, a mode of worship to which philosophical Hinduism, with its tolerant spirit, had no difficulty in reconciling itself.

So the wheel of Hindu life went merrily on, until there arose in the desert of Arabia a power that was destined to revolutionise ideas and to leave a permanent impress.

Mahomet, whilst yet a boy on seeing around him people given to idolatry, to lustful indulgences, and to drunkenness, burned within himself with rage. He saw also Judaism prostrate and Christianity debased. He felt, even as did Moses and Christ, that he was a man with a mission. He decided to deliver his mission to the world, and he chose the members of his own family as the first recipients.

The lecturer was not one of those who believed that the religion of Islam was a religion of the sword.

Washington Irving, in his work on Islam, had asked a pertinent question, namely, 'Where had Islam, in its first stage, found men to wield the sword?' He believed that the success of Mahomedanism was largely due to its simplicity and to its recognition of human weaknesses. He (the Prophet) taught that God was One and only One, that he was His Messenger. He taught also that prayer was absolutely necessary as an uplifting influence, and in order to bring together his followers, if only once in a year, he instituted the pilgrimage to Mecca, for those who could afford it, and recognising that people would amass wealth, he enjoined upon his followers that they set apart a certain portion of it religiously, for charitable purposes. The key-note of Islam was, however, its levelling spirit. It offered equality to all that came within its pale, in the manner that no other religion in the world did.

To this inherent strength was also added the power of the sword. The fanatical raiders who, from time to time, found their way into India, did not hesitate to convert by the sword if they could not do so by persuasion. They more or less overran all parts of India, breaking idols, and although the Rajput valour was at the disposal of Hinduism, it was powerless to afford protection against the Mahomedan in-road.

In keeping with the spirit of Hinduism, an attempt was made at first to bring about reconciliation between the two faiths, and in the city of Benares, there arose a holyman about the 13th century, by name Kabir, who endeavoured, by keeping intact the chief tenets of Hinduism and by borrowing somewhat from Mahomedanism, to bring about a fusion, but the attempt was not quite successful.

The Punjab, through which the Mahomedan conquerors poured into India, and which bore the first brunt, produced Guru Nanak, the founder of the Sikh religion, who drew upon Kabir for his doctrines and added to it militant Hinduism. He offered the olive-branch by respecting the Moslem susceptibilities, but if that were not accepted, he was equally ready to defend Hinduism from the Moslem aggression, and thus Sikhism was a direct result of Islam.

It was well known how brave the Sikh was and what the effect of Mahomedanism on Hinduism was that it gave rise to Sikhism and it brought out one of the chief characteristics of the religion, namely toleration in its true light and fullness. When there were no political influences at work, there was no difficulty about the Hindus and the Mahomedans prejudices of the other, and each following his own faith without let or hindrance.

It was Hinduism that gave Mahomedanism its Akbar, who with unerring insight, recognised the tolerant spirit and adopted it himself in ruling India. Hinduism, moreover, showed its elasticity in that, in spite of the fierce struggle, the classes as well as a large majority of the masses were left totally untouched, and Hinduism arose out of the struggle backed, as we would rise out of a cold bath, with warm glow. The first shock was, no doubt, severely felt, but the Hindu religion soon asserted itself.

The lecturer also mentioned the fakirs and the yogis, and said that they lived almost the same kind of life, although the former belonged to the Islamic faith and the latter to the Hindu faith.

6

Evolution of the Hindus

Hindus are not considered to be the original inhabitants of India. According to Western scholars, the Hindus as well as most of the European people lived at one time in Central Asia. Migrating from there some went to Europe, some to Iran, others moved south-eastwards down into India through the Punjab, and there spread the Aryan religion. The Hindu population in India exceeds two hundred millions. They are called Hindus because they once lived beyond the river Sindhu (Indus).

The Vedas are their oldest scripture. Very devout Hindus believe that the Vedas are of divine origin and without beginning. Western scholars hold these were composed before 2000 B.C. The famous Mr. Tilak[1] of Poona has shown that the Vedas must be at least 10,000 years old. The main thing that distinguishes the Hindus is their belief that the *Brahman* or oversoul is all-pervading. What we all have to attain is *moksha* or liberation, *moksha* here meaning freeing oneself from the evil

[1] Bal Gangadhar Tilak.

of birth and death and merging in the *Brahman*. Humility and even-mindedness are the chief qualities of their ethics; while caste reigns supreme in their temporal affairs.

The Hindu religion underwent its first trial on the advent of Lord Buddha. The Buddha was himself the son of a king. He is said to have been born before 600 B.C. At that time the Hindus were under the glamour of the outward form of their religion, and the Brahmins had, out of selfishness, abandoned their true function of defending the Hindu faith. Lord Buddha was moved to pity when he saw his religion reduced to such a plight. He renounced the world and started doing penance. He spent several years in devout contemplation and ultimately suggested some reform in the Hindu religion. His piety greatly affected the minds of the Brahmins, and the killing of animals for sacrifice was stopped to a great extent. It cannot, therefore, be said that the Buddha founded a new or different religion. But those who came after him gave his teachings the identity of a separate religion. King Ashoka the Great sent missionaries to different lands for the propagation of Buddhism, and spread that religion in Ceylon (now Sri Lanka), China, Burma (now Myanmar) and other countries.

A distinctive beauty of Hinduism was revealed during this process: no one was converted to Buddhism by force. People's minds were sought to be influenced only by discussion and argument and mainly by the very pure conduct of the preachers themselves. It may be said that, in India at any rate, Hinduism and Buddhism were but one, and that even today the fundamental principles of both are identical.

The Birth of Prophet Mohammed

We have seen that Buddhism had a salutary effect on Hinduism, that the champions of the latter were aroused by its impact.

A thousand years ago, the Hindu religion came under another influence more profound. Hazrat Mahomed was born 1300 years ago. He saw moral anarchy rampant in Arabia. Judaism was struggling for survival; Christianity was not able to gain a foothold in the land; and the people were given to licence and self-indulgence. Mahomed felt all this to be improper. It caused him mental agony; and in the name of God, he determined to make them realise their miserable condition. His feeling was so intense that he was able immediately to impress the people around him with his fervour, and Islam spread very rapidly.

Zeal or passion, then, is a great speciality, a mighty force, of Islam. It has been the cause of many good deeds, and sometimes of bad ones too. A thousand years ago the army of Ghazni invaded India in order to spread Islam. Hindu idols were broken and the invasions advanced as far as Somnath. While, on the other, unfolding the real merit of Islam — the Islamic principle that, all those who embraced Islam were equals made such a favourable impression on the lower classes that hundreds of thousands of Hindus accepted that faith, and there was great commotion in the whole community.

Kabir was born in Banaras. He thought that, according to Hindu philosophy, there could be no distinction between a Hindu and a Muslim. Both of them, if they did good works, would find a place in heaven. Idolatry was not an essential part of Hinduism. Reasoning thus, he attempted to bring about a synthesis between Hinduism and Islam; but it did not have much effect, and his became no more than a distinct sect, and it exists even today.

Some years later, Guru Nanak was born in the Punjab; he accepted the reasoning of Kabir and made a similar attempt to fuse the two religions. But while doing so, he felt that

Hinduism should be defended against Islam, if necessary with the sword. This gave rise to Sikhism, and produced the Sikh warriors. The result of all this is that, despite the prevalence of Hinduism and Islam as the two principal religions of India today, both the communities live together in peace and amity and are considerate enough not to hurt one another's feelings save for the bitterness caused by political machinations and excitement. There is very little difference between a Hindu yogi and a Muslim fakir.

Jesus Christ, the Prophet

While Islam and Hinduism were thus vying with each other, the Christians landed at the port of Goa about 500 years ago, and set about converting Hindus to Christianity. They also partly resorted to force and (converted) partly through persuasion. Some of their ministers were exceedingly tender-hearted and kind, rather one would call them saintly. Like the fakirs they made a deep impression on the lower classes of Hindu society. But later, when Christianity and Western civilisation came to be associated, the Hindus began to look upon that religion with disfavour. And today, we see few Hindus embracing Christianity in spite of the fact that the Christians are ruling over a vast kingdom.

Nevertheless, Christianity has had a very considerable influence on Hinduism. Christian priests imparted education of a high order and pointed out some of the glaring defects in Hinduism, with the result that there arose among the Hindus other great teachers, who like Kabir, began to teach the Hindus what was good in Christianity and appealed to them to remove these defects. To this category belonged Raja Ram Mohan Rai[2],

---

2 18th century religious, social and educational reformer; one of the founder of Brahmo Samaj.

Devendranath Tagore[3], and Keshab Chandra Sen[4]. In Western India we had Dayanand Saraswati[5]. And the numerous reformist associations like the Brahmo Samaj and the Arya Samaj that have sprung up in India today are doubtless the result of Christian influence. Again, Madame Blavatsky[6] came to India, told both Hindus and the Muslims of evils of Western civilisation and asked them to beware of becoming enamoured of it.

Tenets of Hinduism

Thus, we have seen how there have been three assaults on Hinduism, coming from Buddhism, Islam and then Christianity, but how on the whole it came out of them unscathed. It has tried to imbibe whatever was good in each of these religions.

We should, however, know what the followers of this religion, Hinduism, believe.

This is what they believe: God exists. He is without beginning, immaculate, and without any attribute or form. He is omnipresent and omnipotent. His original form is *Brahman.* It neither does, nor causes to be done. It does not govern. It is bliss incarnate, and by it all this is sustained. The soul exists, and is distinct from the body. It also is without a beginning, without birth. Between its original form and the *Brahman,* there is no distinction. But it takes on, from time to time a body as a result of *karma* or the power of *maya,* and goes on being born again

3 Hindu philosopher and religious reformer active in Brahmo Samaj.

4 19th century Hindu philosopher, social reformer and member of Brahmo Samaj.

5 Spiritual leader and social reformer of the 19th century; founded Arya Samaj.

6 Russian-German occutlist who established Theosophical society.

and again into high or low species in accordance with the good or bad deeds performed by it.

To be free from the cycle of birth and death and be merged in *Brahman* is *moksha* or liberation. The way to achieve this *moksha* is to do pure and good deeds; to have compassion for all living beings, and to live in truth. Even after reaching this stage, one does not attain liberation, for one has to enjoy embodied existence as a consequence of one's good deeds as well.

One has, therefore, to go a step further. We will, however, have to continue to act, only we should not cherish any attachment to our actions. Action should be undertaken for its own sake, without an eye on the fruit. In short, everything should be dedicated to God. We should not cherish, even in a dream, the feeling of pride that we do or can do anything. We should look upon all equally. These are the beliefs or tenets of Hinduism, but there admittedly exist a number of schools. Also, there have arisen a few factions or sects resulting from (differences in) secular practices. But we need not consider them on the present occasion.

All religions teach that we should all live together in love and mutual kindness.

7

How May Scriptures Be Interpreted[1]

I have a correspondent who always brings me to book for the slightest negligence on my part. He is evidently a regular student of *Young India,* but no blind admirer. Here is a candid but friendly critic, and, if he sees something good in my writings, he detects errors also. One of his letters drawing attention to a possible inconsistency in my writings has long remained in file. One portion of it deals with the definition of '*Sanatana Hindu*'. Here is the letter:

'You have often declared yourself a *sanatana* Hindu, defining one as a believer in the Vedas, smritis etc., and laid emphasis on the institution of castes by birth as legitimately following from the 'scriptures'. Of course you limit the number of castes to the supposed pristine four. (I say 'supposed pristine' advisedly, for, even as early as the times of the production of Manu('s) and other *smritis,* there had been already so many castes evolved out of and recognized over and above the ideal four, although, be it noted, inter-dining and inter-marriage amongst them all had

[1] Originally published under the title *Sanatana Hindu* in *Young India.*

not yet come to be interdicted.) Now the fourth or, last in order of the 'fundamental' castes, is the Sudra, which is debarred by those very 'scriptures' a belief in which you regard as the sine qua non of a *sanatana* Hindu, as well as by their 'twice-born' professors, from studying or reciting the divine Vedas including the Gayatri, a recitation of which you mention as obligatory upon a *sanatana* Hindu (without distinction of caste).

So the question arises: How can anyone (e.g., a Sudra) be said to belong to a religion (viz., Hinduism as defined by you), if the mere reading, reciting or even the hearing of its scripture is tabooed to him, as though it were a sacrilege? How can you expect a man to be a swimmer without letting him step into water?

Either one who is born a Sudra cannot be a *sanatana* Hindu in your sense, or else a *sanatana* Hindu must be something very different from what you define one to be. (I refer you to your old article on 'Hinduism' in 1921 and your address to the cow conference at Belgaum as printed in *Young India*, Jan 1, 1925). I for one, whom a Brahmin birth, cannot glorify in the name of 'Hindu' so long as an exemplar of real *sanatana* dharma like you permit the term to cover a bundle of contradictions like the one I have pointed out.

Lastly, in view of your mention of Gayatri, may I humbly inquire whether you have in your 'twice-born' life never omitted to include the Gayatri in your daily prayers?'

I am not a literalist. Therefore, I try to understand the spirit of the various scriptures of the world. I apply the test of truth and *ahimsa* laid down by these very scriptures for interpretation. I reject what is inconsistent with that test, and I appropriate all that is consistent with it.

The story of a Sudra having been punished by Ramachandra for daring to learn the Vedas I reject as an interpolation. And in

The chief value of Hinduism lies in holding the actual belief that all life (not only human beings, but all sentient beings) is one.

any event, I worship Rama, the perfect being of my conception, not a historical person, facts about whose life may vary with the progress of new historical discoveries and researches.

Tulsidas had nothing to do with the Rama of history. Judged by historical test, his *Ramayana* would be fit for the scrap heap. As a spiritual experience, his book is almost unrivalled, at least for me. And then, too, I do not swear by every word that is to be found in so many editions published as the *Ramayana* of Tulsidas. It is the spirit running through the book that holds me spellbound.

I cannot myself subscribe to the prohibition against Sudras learning the Vedas. Indeed, in my opinion, at the present moment, we are all predominantly Sudras as long as we are serfs. Knowledge cannot be the prerogative of any class or section. But I can conceive the impossibility of people assimilating higher or subtler truths, unless they have undergone preliminary training, even as those who have not made preliminary preparations are quite unfit to breathe the rarefied atmosphere in high altitudes, or those who have no preliminary training in simple mathematics are unfit to understand or assimilate higher geometry or algebra.

Lastly, I believe in certain healthy conventions. There is a convention surrounding the recitation of the Gayatri. The convention is that it should be recited only at stated times and after ablutions performed in the prescribed manner. As I believe in those conventions, and as I am not able always to conform to them, for years past I have followed the later saints, and therefore have satisfied myself with the *dwadashamantra* of the *Bhagavata* or the still simpler formula of Tulsidas and a few selections from the *Gita* and other works, and a few *bhajans* in Prakrit. These are my daily spiritual food — my Gayatri. They give me all the peace and solace I need from day to day.

8

Who is a Sanatani Hindu?

It has been asked why I call myself an orthodox *sanatani* Hindu and why I regard myself as a *Vaishnava.* I think I should answer these questions.

The answer will cover the definition of a *sanatani* Hindu and include a complete description of a *Vaishnava.*

According to my belief, a Hindu is anyone who, born in a Hindu family in India, accepts the Vedas, the Upanishads and the Puranas as holy books; who has faith in the five *yamas* of truth, non-violence, etc., and practises them to the best of his ability; who believes an the existence of the *atman* and the *paramatman* (supreme self), and believes, further, that the *atman* (self) is never born and never dies but, through incarnation in the body passes from existence to existence and is capable of attaining *moksha;* who believes that *moksha* is the supreme end of human striving and believes in *varnashrama* and cow-protection.

Whoever, besides believing in all these, has been born in a family belonging to the *Vaishnava* sect and has not forsaken the *Vaishnava* way; who possesses in some measure the qualities described in Narasinh Mehta's[1] devotional song entitled '*Vaishnavajana*' and strives to cultivate these qualities in perfection is a *Vaishnava.*

It is my firm belief that I possess in a large measure the characteristics described by me and I have been striving to strengthen them. I do not, therefore, hesitate to call myself with all firmness, though humbly, a strict *sanatani* Hindu and a *Vaishnava.*

I believe that the most important outward form of Hinduism is cow-protection. I regard the Hindu world as impotent because at present not a single Hindu is capable of giving that protection. Among these impotent people, I believe myself to be the least impotent. I do not believe that there can be anybody else who has systematically exerted himself as much as I have done, and am still doing, for the protection of cows or who feels for the cow and its progeny as much as I do. As long as the Hindus in India show no kindness to the cow, as long as they themselves torture cattle in many ways, as long as they have not succeeded in winning the regard of Muslims and persuading them to stop, out of their regard, the slaughter of cows, and as long as they tolerate the killing of cows by the English and salute the British flag, I shall believe that the Brahmin and the Kshatriya spirit has vanished from Hinduism. Therefore, though born a Vaisya, I am ever active in the duties of both.

~

I believe that the essence of Hinduism is truth and non-violence. I have not seen anyone among those whom I know

[1] 1414-1479; saint poet of Gujarati admired by Gandhiji for disregarding the common prejudice against the so-called untouchables.

respecting truth so scrupulously as I have been doing right from my childhood. The active manifestation of non-violence is love — absence of ill will. I firmly believe that I am overflowing with love. I have not felt ill will against anyone even in a dream. I entertain no such feeling towards Dyer[2], his wicked deeds notwithstanding. Wherever I have seen misery or injustice, I have felt troubled in my soul.

The central principle of Hinduism is that of *moksha.* I am ever striving for it. All my activities are for *moksha.* I have as much faith in the existence of the *atman* and in its immortality as I am certain of the existence of my body and its transience.

For these reasons, I am happy to declare myself a staunch *sanatani* Hindu.

~

If anybody asks me whether I have made any deep study of the *shastras,* I would say that I have and I have not. I have not studied them from a scholar's point of view. My knowledge of Sanskrit is almost nil; even of the translations available in modern Indian languages, I have read only a few. I cannot claim to have fully read even a single Veda. Nevertheless, I have understood the *shastras* from the point of view of dharma. I have grasped their real meaning. I know that one can attain *moksha* without reading the Vedas.

I have found the right method for reading — for understanding — the *shastras.* If any injunction in a *shastra* is opposed to truth, non-violence and *brahmacharya,* it is unauthentic, whichever the *shastra* in which it is found. The *shastras* are not above reason. We can reject any *shastras* which reason cannot follow. I have read through only the Upanishads.

---

[2] General Dyer who fired on Hindus on Baisakhi.

I have also read some among them which my reason could not follow. I did not, therefore, accept them as having any authority. Many poets have told us in their poems that anyone who sticks to the letter of the shastras is a pedant. Teachers like Shankaracharya on the Upanishads, *Brahmasutras* and the *Bhagavad Gita* have given the essence of the shastras in single sentences, and the sum and substance of it all is that one should cultivate bhakti towards God and attain *jnana* (enlightenment), and thereby attain *moksha.* Akha Bhagat has said:

Live as you please.
  Attain God anyhow, somehow.

That *shastra* which teaches me drinking liquor, eating meat and wicked ways cannot be called a *shastra.*

Much that is the very opposite of dharma is going on in the name of the smritis. By trying to follow the letter of the smritis and other such works, we make ourselves fit for hell. Deluded by these, people who call themselves Hindus give themselves up to licence and become ready to commit or make others commit rape on young girls.

~

We now have before us the important question of what, in all the *shastras,* we should regard as interpolations, what as acceptable and what as deserving to be rejected. If there had not been, as I have stated above, a total extinction of the Brahmin spirit, we could have consulted a Brahmin who had purified himself by following the disciplines of *yama-niyama* and acquired a good measure of *jnana.* In the absence of such Brahmins, the path of *bhakti* rules supreme at present. When we have brought about self-purification by non-co-operating with the present

Government in which the sins of hypocrisy, pretension, pride, worldliness and so on, reveal themselves in numerous ways, then perhaps we shall get a cultured person who can give us the essence of the *shastras.*

Till then we, the common people, may cling to the essentials with a simple faith and live our lives in *bhakti* to God. I see no other way.

'There can be no *jnana* without a guru' is a golden maxim. But it is very difficult to find a guru, and it would not be proper to accept any person as a guru in the absence of a good one and so drown ourselves right in the middle of our voyage across. How can a man who knows no swimming save others? Even if such swimmers exist in modern times, they are not a common sight.

9

Varnashrama: A Critical Interpretation[1]

A friend has asked Gandhi three questions in a most humble spirit, and one of the questions related to *varnashrama.* The question and Gandhi's reply are reproduced here:

Question: You regard the four divisions of castes as based on birth. You also believe that a man's caste does not prevent him from doing the duties attaching to other castes and that any man, irrespective of his birth, may have the qualities of a Brahmin, or a Kshatriya or a Sudra.

If this is the case, where is the use of maintaining this division, and consequently, an order of superiority and inferiority? Why should the accident of birth make a man a Brahmin or a Kshatriya or a Sudra? Why attach so much importance to birth?

[1] The Gujarati original of this appeared in *Navajivan,* Jan 17, 1926. This is a translation by Mahadev Desai. Originally published under the title *Varnashrama* in *Collected Works of M K Gandhi,* Vol 33, Sept 25, 1925-Feb 10, 1926, pp 408-409.

Gandhi's response: In accepting the fourfold division, I am simply accepting the laws of Nature, taking for granted what is inherent in human nature, and the law of heredity.

We are born with some of the traits of our parents. The fact that a human being is born only in the human species shows that some characteristics, i.e., caste is determined by birth. There is scope enough for freedom of the will inasmuch as we can to a certain extent reform some of our inherited characteristics. It is not possible in one birth entirely to undo the results of our past doings, and in the light of it, it is in every way right and proper to regard him as a Brahmin who is born of Brahmin parents. A Brahmin may by doing the deeds of a Sudra become a Sudra in this very birth, but the world loses nothing in continuing to treat him as a Brahmin.

Caste as it exists today is no doubt a travesty of the original fourfold division which only defined men's different callings. And this trifling with it has been its undoing. But how can I, for that reason, discard the law of Nature which I see being fulfilled at every step? I know that if I discard it, I would be rid of a lot of trouble. But that would be an idle short-cut.

I have declared from the house-tops that a man's caste is no matter for pride, that no superiority attaches to any of the four divisions. A true Brahmin will feel it an honour to serve the lowliest of Sudras. In fact a Brahmin, to be a Brahmin, should have the qualities of a Kshatriya, a Vaisya and a Sudra plus his own. Only he should predominantly be a man of divine knowledge. But caste today is in the crucible, and only heaven knows, or perhaps the Brahmins know, the final result.

~

Varnashrama is, in my opinion, inherent in human nature, and Hinduism has simply reduced it to a science. It does attach to birth. A man cannot change his *varna* by choice. Not to abide by one's *varna* is to disregard the law of heredity. The division, however, into innumerable castes is an unwarranted liberty taken with the doctrine. The four divisions are all-sufficing.

I have always believed that there are no more than four *varnas* (castes). I believe that one acquires one's caste by birth. One who is born in a Brahmin family dies a Brahmin. If he becomes a non-Brahmin through his qualities of character, his Brahmin body does not cease to be such. A Brahmin who does not follow the Brahmin dharma may be born, according to his deeds, as a Sudra, or even as an animal. A Vaisya like me who follows the dharma of a Brahmin and of a Kshatriya, if he has to be born again, may well be a Brahmin or a Kshatriya in the next birth. So far as this life is concerned, he will remain a Vaisya, and rightly so.

From time to time persons belonging to other faiths have been absorbed by Hinduism, but they were not known as Hindus during their lifetime. The Hindu world is like a sea. All refuse that finds its way into its bosom gets purified, settles down.

This has happened again and again. People from Italy, Greece and elsewhere came in and were absorbed by Hinduism, but they were not converted by anyone to Hinduism. Merely in course of ages, the numbers have risen and fallen. Unlike Christianity or Islam, Hinduism does not invite persons of other faiths to join its fold; it enjoins all to follow their own religions. Sister Nivedita[2], for instance, embraced Hinduism but

[2] An Anglo-Irish social worker who became a disciple of Swami Vivekanand.

we do not think of her as a Hindu, nor do we boycott or slight her in any way. There is no question of anybody embracing Hinduism. Everybody can practise Hinduism.

Varnashrama is a law. The practical question is the caste system. Castes are subject to increase and decrease (in number). They come into existence and they disappear. Only the man himself can leave Hinduism, though he may be expelled from the caste. Ex-communication by the caste is a mode of punishment and ought to be available to every community.

It is certainly necessary that the numerous castes should become fewer, and this can be brought about by the councils of the various castes without injury to Hinduism. If the various divisions of *banias* (broadly refers to *vaisyas*) were together and their members marry among themselves, that will not harm religion in any way.

~

Hinduism reached the highest limit of self-restraint. It is undoubtedly a religion of renunciation of the flesh so that the spirit may be set free.

Salvation is freedom from birth and hence death also. Prohibition against inter-marriage and inter-dining is essential for a rapid evolution of the soul. But this self-denial is no test of *varna.* A Brahmin may remain a Brahmin, though he may dine with his Sudra brother, if he has not left off his duty of service by knowledge. It follows from what I have said above, that restraint in matters of marriage and dining is not based upon notions of superiority. A Hindu who refuses to dine with another from a sense of superiority misrepresents his dharma.

10

What has Hinduism Done for Us?[1]

The following question was put to Gandhiji after his talk at one of the places during his tour in South India.

Question: We see you swear by Hinduism. May we know what Hinduism has done for us? Is it not a legacy of ugly and superstitious practices?

Gandhi's response: I thought I had made it clear already. Varnashrama dharma itself is a unique contribution of Hinduism to the world. Hinduism has saved us from *bhaya,* i.e. peril. If Hinduism had not come to my rescue, the only course for me would have been suicide. I remain a Hindu because Hinduism is a leaven which makes the world worth living in. From Hinduism was born Buddhism. What we see today is not pure Hinduism, but often a parody of it. Otherwise it would require no pleading from me in its behalf, but would speak for itself, even as if I was absolutely pure I would not need to speak

[1] From '*Brahmana-Non-Brahmana* Question' — by Mahadev Desai.

to you. God does not speak with His tongue, and man, in the measure that he comes near God, becomes like God. Hinduism teaches me that my body is a limitation of the power of the soul within.

Just as in the West they have made wonderful discoveries in things material, similarly Hinduism has made still more marvellous discoveries in things of religion, of the spirit, of the soul. But we have no eye for these great and fine discoveries. We are dazzled by the material progress that Western science has made. I am not enamoured of that progress. In fact, it almost seems as though God in His wisdom had prevented India from progressing along those lines so that it might fulfil its special mission of resisting the onrush of materialism. After all, there is something in Hinduism that has kept it alive up till now. It has witnessed the fall of Babylonia, Syrian, Persian and Egyptian civilization. Cast a look round you. Where is Rome and where is Greece? Can you find today anywhere the Italy of Gibbon, or rather the ancient Rome, for Rome was Italy? Go to Greece. Where is the world-famous Attic civilization? Then come to India, let one go through the most ancient records and then look round you and you would be constrained to say, 'Yes, I see here ancient India still living.' True, there are dung-heaps too, here and there, but there are rich treasures buried under them. And the reason why it has survived is that the end which Hinduism set before it was not development along material but spiritual lines.

Among its many contributions the idea of man's identity with the dump creation is a unique one. To me cow-worship is a great idea which is capable of expansion. Its freedom from the modern proselytization is also to me a precious thing. It needs no preaching. It says, 'Live the life.' It is my business, it is your business to live the life, and then we will leave its influence on ages. Then take its contribution in men; Ramanuja, Chaitanya[2], Ramkrishna[3], not to speak of the more modern names, have left their impress on Hinduism. Hinduism is by no means a spent force or a dead religion.

Then there is the contribution of the four Ashramas, again a unique contribution. There is nothing like it in the whole world. The Catholics have the order of celibates corresponding to *Brahmacharis,* but not as an institution, whereas in India every boy had to go through the first Ashrama. What a grand conception it was! Today our eyes are dirty, thoughts dirtier and bodies dirtiest of all, because we are denying Hinduism.

There is yet another thing I have not mentioned. Max Muller said forty years ago that it was dawning on Europe that transmigration is not a theory, but a fact. Well, it is entirely the contribution of Hinduism.

Today Varnashrama dharma and Hinduism are misinterpreted and denied by its votaries. The remedy is not destruction, but correction. Let us reproduce in ourselves the true Hindu spirit, and then ask whether it satisfies the soul or not.

---

[2] Chaitanya Mahaprabhu (1486-1534) was a social reformer in eastern India in the 16th century.

[3] Popularly known as Ramakrishna Paramahamsa (1836-1886) was a famous mystic of the 19th century India.

The reason why Hinduism
has survived is that the
end which it sets before it was
not development along
material but spiritual lines.

11

No Contradiction between the Jain & the Vedic Doctrine

Purushottam Gandhi writing from Rajkot asked Gandhiji three questions:

1. What is the difference between the so-called atheism of the Jains and the theism of the *Gita?*
2. If God is not a doer, who dispenses grace? Is prayer anything more than the expression of a person's wishes?
3. What do you mean when you say that Truth is God?

To him Gandhiji replied as follows:

I do not think there is any contradiction between the Jain and the Vedic doctrine. They are only different ways of looking at the same thing. The God of Vedic Hinduism is doer as well as non-doer. God pervades the universe and is therefore a doer, but He is a non-doer inasmuch as action does not affect Him, and He has not to enjoy the fruit of action. The universe is not the result of any karma (action) of God in the sense in which you use that word. Therefore there is no discrepancy in the *Gita* verses quoted by you.

Remember that the *Gita* is a poem. God neither says nor does anything. He did not say anything to Arjuna. The conversation between the Lord and Arjuna is imaginary. I do not think there was any such conversation between the Krishna and the Arjuna of history.

There is nothing improper or untruthful in the setting of the *Gita.* There was a custom of casting religious books into such a shape, and we cannot find fault with any cultured individual even today who employs such a vehicle for his ideas. The Jains put it logically, unpoetically and drily and said that there is no Creator of the universe. There is nothing wrong in saying so. However mankind cannot live by logic alone, but needs poetry. Therefore, even the Jain rationalists found it necessary to have temples, images and similar aids for the spirit of man, which are ruled out by the cold logic.

In answering your first question I have in effect also answered the second. Grace is the diction of poetry. Devotion *(bhakti)* is itself poetry. But poetry is no improper or inferior or unnecessary thing. On the contrary it is badly needed. Science would tell us that water is a chemical compound of hydrogen and oxygen, but in the language of poetry water is the gift of God. Understanding such poetry is an essential element of life, while ignorance of the chemical composition of water does not matter in the least. It is perfectly logical to say that whatever happens is the fruit of action. But 'impenetrable is the secret of action' (Gita IV, 17).

We mortals are so constituted that we cannot know all the causative factors of even a very ordinary event. We are therefore perfectly right in saying that nothing happens except by the will and the grace of God. Again the body is a prison for the soul, who is like the air enclosed by a jar. The air in the jar is ineffective so long as it thinks itself to be different from the atmosphere. In the same way the soul imprisoned in the body will be unable to draw upon the Reservoir of Power that is God so long as she imagines herself to be a doer. Therefore to say that whatever happens happens by the will of God is to state a matter of fact, and such humility befits a seeker of truth.

A lover of truth entertains only righteous wishes which are bound to be fulfilled. Our prayers bear fruit for the world to the extent that our soul is grounded in truth. The universe is not different from us, and we are not different from the universe. We are all members of one another, and influence one another by our actions. Actions here include thoughts, so that not a single thought is without its effect. Therefore we must cultivate the habit of always thinking good thoughts.

I say that truth is God not because God is without form and so is truth, but because truth is the only comprehensive attribute of God. Other attributes are only partial expressions of the reality that is God. The Gujarati word *Ishwara* (the Lord) is also a descriptive epithet of God but as it literally means ruler, it sounds quite insipid. Thinking of God as the King of kings does not satisfy the intellect. Such a line of thought may generate a kind of fear in our minds, so that we are afraid of committing sin and are encouraged in doing meritorious deeds. But merit acquired out of fear almost ceases to be merit. Let us do good for its own sake, and not in order to win a reward.

Pondering over the matter like this, I found that 'God is truth' is an incomplete sentence. 'Truth is God' is the fullest expression of our meaning in so far as it can be set forth in human speech. We arrive at the same conclusion if we consider the etymology of the word *satya* (truth), which is derived from *sat. Sat* means eternal. That which exists at all times is truth. It alone is, everything else is not. But while we learn to recognize

The central principle of
Hinduism is that of *moksha*.
To be free from the cycle of
birth and death and be merged
in *Brahman* is *moksha*
or liberation.

God as truth, we must not allow our faith to weaken. On the other hand it should grow stronger. This is my experience.

By looking upon truth as God we steer clear of quite a number of dangers. We lose all interest in seeing or hearing about miracles. Seeing God is difficult to understand; but seeing truth presents no such difficulty. Seeing truth is indeed a hard task, but as we approach nearer and nearer to truth we catch a glimpse of the God of truth, so that we hope to have a full view in His good time and our faith also burns brighter and brighter.

12

The True Meaning of Yajna

Yajna means an act directed to the welfare of others, done without desiring any return for it, whether of a temporal or spiritual nature. 'Act' here must be taken in its widest sense, and includes thought and word, as well as deed. 'Others' embraces not only humanity, but all life.

Therefore, and also from the standpoint of *ahimsa*, it is not *yajna* to sacrifice lower animals even with a view to the service of humanity. It does not matter that animal sacrifice is alleged to find a place in the *Vedas*. It is enough for us that such sacrifice cannot stand the fundamental tests of truth and non-violence.

I readily admit my incompetence in *Vedic* scholarship. But the incompetence, so far as this subject is concerned, does not worry me, because even if the practice of animal sacrifice be proved to have been a feature of Vedic society, it can form no precedent for a votary of *ahimsa*.

Again a primary sacrifice must be an act, which conduces the most to the welfare of the greatest number in the widest area, and which can be performed by the largest number of men and women with the least trouble. It will *not* therefore, be a *yajna*, much less a *mahayajna*, to wish or to do ill to any one else, even in order to serve a so-called higher interest. And the *Gita* teaches, and experience testifies, that all action that cannot come under the category of *yajna* promotes bondage.

The world cannot subsist for a single moment without *yajna* in this sense, and therefore the *Gita*, after having dealt with true wisdom in the second chapter, takes up in the third the means of attaining it, and declares in so many words, that *yajna* came with the Creation itself. This body, therefore, has been given us, only in order that we may serve all creation with it. And, therefore, says the *Gita*, he who eats without offering *yajna* eats stolen food. Every single act of one who would lead a life of purity should be in the nature of *yajna*.

Yajna having come to us with our birth, we are debtors all our lives, and thus forever bound to serve the universe. And even as a bondslave receives food, clothing and so on from the master whom he serves, so should we gratefully accept such gifts as may be assigned to us by the Lord of the universe. What we receive must be called a gift; for as debtors we are entitled to no consideration for the discharge of our obligations. Therefore we may not blame the Master, if we fail to get it. Our body is His, to be cherished or cast away according to His will. This is not a matter for complaint or even pity; on the contrary, it is natural and even a pleasant and desirable state, if only we realize our proper place in God's scheme. We do indeed need strong faith, if we would experience this supreme bliss. 'Do not worry in the least about yourself, leave all worry to God.' — this appears to be the commandment in all religions.

This need not frighten any one. He who devotes himself to service with a clear conscience will day by day grasp the necessity for it in greater measure, and will continually grow richer in

Yajna means an act directed to the welfare of others, done without desiring any return for it, whether of a temporal or spiritual nature.

faith. The path of service can hardly be trodden by one, who is not prepared to renounce self-interest, and to recognize the conditions of his birth. Consciously or unconsciously every one of us does render some service or other.

Yajna is not *yajna* if one feels it to be burdensome or annoying. Self-indulgence leads to destruction, and renunciation to immortality. Joy has no independent existence. It depends upon our attitude to life. One man will enjoy theatrical scenery, another the ever new scenes which unfold themselves in the sky. Joy, therefore, is a matter of individual and national education. We shall relish things which we have been taught to relish as children. And illustrations can be easily cited of different national tastes.

Again, many sacrificers imagine that they are free to receive from the people everything they need, and many things they do not need, because they are rendering disinterested service. Directly this idea sways a man, he ceases to be a servant, and becomes a tyrant over the people.

One who would serve will not waste a thought upon his own comforts, which he leaves to be attended to or neglected by his Master on high. He will not therefore encumber himself with everything that comes his way; he will take only what he strictly needs and leave the rest. He will be calm, free from anger and unruffled in mind even if he finds himself inconvenienced. His service, like virtue, is its own reward, and he will rest content with it.

Again, one dare not be negligent in service, or be behindhand with it. He, who thinks that one must be diligent only in one's personal business, and unpaid public business may be done in any way and at any time one chooses, has still to learn the very rudiments of the science of sacrifice. Voluntary service of others demands the best of which one is capable, and must take precedence over service of self. In fact, the pure devotee consecrates himself to the service of humanity without any reservation whatever.

13

Importance of Tapas

There are instances of *tapas* (penance) at every step in Hindu mythology. Parvati desired to win Shankara and she took to *tapas.* Siva did something wrong and so he undertook *tapas.* Vishwamitra[1] was the very incarnation of *tapas.* When Rama went into exile, Bharata plunged into yoga discipline, practised austere *tapas* and wore out his body.

God cannot test man in any other manner. If the soul is different from the body, it should remain, blissful even when the body is tormented. Food is nourishment for the body, whereas knowledge and meditation are sustenance to the soul. Everyone has to realize this for himself as and when occasion arises.

If, however, the *tapas* is accompanied by faith, devotion and humility, then all that austerity becomes a futile exercise. It also becomes hypocrisy. A devotee of God who enjoys eating his meal is a thousand times better than such an ascetic.

---

[1] One of the most venerated *rishis* or sages of ancient India; one of the *Brahmrishi.*

I have not the strength today to narrate the story of *tapas* but I may state that I cannot possibly live without *tapas.* Once again I am destined to plunge into the stormy ocean. Please, God, know that I am humble and protect me.

14

Brahmacharya: Search for the Brahman[1]

It is not easy to write on this subject. But my own experience is so wide that I always wish to give some of it to the reader. Many letters which I have received have strengthened that wish. A friend asks: 'What is *brahmacharya?* Is perfect observance of *brahmacharya* possible? If it is, do you observe it so?'

The full and correct meaning of *brahmacharya* is search for the *brahman.* As the *Brahman* is immanent in everyone, it can be known through contemplation and the inner illumination resulting from it. This illumination is not possible without complete control over the senses. Hence, *brahmacharya* means control in thought, speech and action of all senses, at all places and at all times.

The man or woman who observes such perfect brahmacharya is totally free from disease and, therefore, he or she lives ever in the presence of God, is like God. I have no doubt that complete

---

[1] Originally published under the title *Brahmacharya* in *Navajivan.*

observance of such *brahmacharya* in thought, speech and action is possible.

I regret to say that I have not attained to the state of such perfect *brahmacharya.* I am striving every moment to reach it. I have not given up the hope of attaining that state in this very life. I have acquired control over my body. I can guard myself during the waking state. I have acquired fairly good control over speech.

I have yet to gain good enough control over my thoughts. When I begin to think about a certain matter, I may have thoughts about other matters too, resulting in a constant clashing of thoughts. Even so, in my waking moments I am able to stop such clash of thoughts. I have attained a state, it can be claimed, in which ugly thoughts at any rate do not trouble me. But I have less control over my thoughts during sleep. In that state, all manner of thoughts come to me, even strange dreams, and sometimes desire for indulgences familiar to the body also wakes up in me. When the thoughts are unclean, there may be involuntary discharge too. This condition is possible only in a life troubled by desire. The disturbances in my thoughts are becoming weaker, but I have not ceased altogether. Had I acquired complete mastery over my thoughts, I would not have been, during the last ten years, afflicted with the three diseases of pleurisy, dysentery and appendicitis[2].

I believe that the body encasing a healthy *atman* is bound to be healthy. Hence, as the *atman* becomes healthier — is less and less troubled by desire — the body too becomes healthier.

Such a wonderful state is certainly difficult to attain. Else I would have reached it, for, as my *atman* testifies, I would not

[2] Gandhiji had an attack of pleurisy in October 1914, of dysentery in August 1918 and of appendicitis in January 1924.

be remiss in taking all measures necessary for attaining it. There is nothing in this world which can keep me from striving for it. But it is not easy for everyone to undo the accumulated effects of his past.

So far I have discussed *brahmacharya* in its comprehensive meaning. The conventional and commonly accepted meaning of *brahmacharya* is, simply, control of the sex impulse in thought, speech and action. This view of it is realistic, for observance of *brahmacharya* in this sense is believed to be very difficult. Control over the palate has not been equally emphasized, and that has made control of the sex impulse more difficult. It has become almost impossible. Again, the experience of doctors tells us that a person whose body is weakened by disease is more troubled by sex desire and this is an additional reason why observance of *brahmacharya* seems difficult to our disease-ridden people.

I have referred above to a body being lean but healthy. No one should take me to mean that one need not develop physical strength. I have merely expressed, in my imperfect language, my idea about *brahmacharya* in its finest aspect. What I have said may possibly be misunderstood. Anyone who wishes to acquire complete control over all the senses has no choice, ultimately, but to welcome his body becoming lean. When blind love of the body and attachment for it decline, no desire for physical strength will be left.

But the body of a *brahmachari* who has conquered sex desire ought to be strong and glowing with vigour. Even the observance of this *brahmacharya* raises one above the common level. He who does not feel physical urge even in a dream deserves to be honoured by the world. There is little doubt that it is easy for such a one to exercise self-control in other matters.

About *brahmacharya* in this sense, another friend writes:

> My condition is pitiable. Whether I am chanting the name of God, whether I am in the office or walking in the street, whether I am reading at night or working, I get those very thoughts. What should I do to control my thoughts? How can one develop the same regard for every woman as one has for one's mother? What should be done so that the eyes will shine with nothing but pure affection? What is the way to be free from evil thoughts? I have preserved with me your article[3] on *brahmacharya*, but in this place it is of no help to me at all.

This is a touching plight. Many find themselves in such a condition. But there is no cause for apprehension as long as one's mind wrestles with thoughts of that kind. If the eyes offend, they should be closed. If the ears offend, they should be plugged with cotton wool. It is a good habit to walk with one's eyes always on the ground. They will, then, get no opportunity at all to see anything else; One should run away from a place where people are talking obscene things or singing obscene songs. One must acquire control over the palate.

It is my experience that anyone who has not conquered the palate cannot conquer the sex impulse. It is very difficult to conquer the palate. But victory over it is essential for the other victory. One way to conquer the palate is to give up condiments wholly or as far as possible, and another effective way is to keep thinking that we eat merely to keep the body and soul together, and that we would never indulge the palate. We breathe not for the pleasure of breathing, but for taking in air. We drink water to slake thirst and, likewise, we should eat only to satisfy hunger. Right from childhood, our parents develop in us the

[3] Presumably, 'How Celibacy Can Be Observed', Nov 10, 1921.

opposite habit. They spoil us by teaching us to enjoy all manner of delicacies, which they do, not for our nourishment, but to show their love for us. We have to fight such tendencies.

But the golden rule for conquering the sex impulse is to keep repeating the magic name of Rama or some such holy word. Even the *dwadashmantra* serves the same purpose. One may choose the mantra to be chanted as prompted by one's faith. I have suggested the name of Rama because I was initiated into it from my childhood and have always found support in it. Whichever mantra we choose, we must become one with it. Even if other thoughts distract us while we repeat the mantra, I have no doubt at all that anyone who keeps repeating it with faith will succeed ultimately. The mantra will come to be the support of one's life and save one from all dangers. No one should have recourse to such a holy mantra for material gain. The miracle of the mantra lies in preserving our moral purity and everyone who tries will have that experience in a short while.

Of course, we should remember that this mantra is not to be repeated parrot-wise; it should be repeated with one's whole being. The parrot repeats such mantras mechanically; we should do so intelligently, with purpose to keep away unwanted thoughts and with faith in the efficacy of the mantra.

15

The Nature of Atman[1]

Anyone who knows the nature of the *atman* will believe that to be literally so. If the *atman* never perishes, what does it matter that the houses it inhabits perish or that the garments which it puts on wear out and decay?

Moreover, the *atman* is eternally perfect and so it can never lack a house to inhabit. If we but know the truth, it needs none. But all this is true only with reference to oneself.

Question: Do you then believe in the personal immortality of the soul?[2]

Gandhi's reply: Yes, I believe in the immortality of the soul. I would like to give you the analogy of the ocean. The ocean is composed of drops of water, each drop is an entity and yet it is part of the whole, 'the one and the many'. In this ocean of life

1 Letter from M K Gandhi to Premabehan Kantak written on Jan 30, 1932.

2 Interview to Evelyn Wrench, London (On or after Oct 17, 1931).

we are all little drops. My doctrine means that I must identify myself with life, with everything that lives, that I must share the majesty of life in the presence of God. The sum total of this life is God.

16

God is All Things to All Men

To me God is truth and love: God is ethics and morality; God is fearlessness. God is the source of light and life and yet He is above and beyond all these. God is conscience. He is even the atheism of the atheist. For in His boundless love God permits the atheist to live. He is the searcher of hearts: He transcends speech and reason. He knows us and our hearts better than we do ourselves. He does not take us at our word for He knows that we often do not mean it, some knowingly and others unknowingly. He is a personal God to those who need His personal presence. He is embodied to those who need His touch. He is the purest essence. He simply is to those who have faith. He is all things to all men.

He is in us and yet above and beyond us. One may banish the word 'God' but one has no power to banish the Thing itself. What is a solemn affirmation, if it is not same thing as in the name of God? And surely conscience is but a poor and laborious paraphrase of the simple combination of three letters called God. He cannot cease to be because hideous immoralities or inhuman brutalities are committed in His name. He is long suffering. He is patient but He is also terrible. He is the most exacting personage in the world and the world to come. He metes out the same measure to us we mete out to our neighbours — men and brutes. With Him ignorance is no excuse. And withal He is ever forgiving for He always gives us the chance to repent. He is the greatest democrat the world knows, for He leaves us 'unfettered' to make our own choice between evil and good. He is the greatest tyrant ever know, for He often dashes the cup from our lips and under cover of free will leaves us a margin so wholly inadequate as to provide only mirth for Himself at our expense. Therefore it is that Hinduism calls it all His sport — *lila*, or calls it all an illusion — *maya*. We are not, He alone is. And if we will be, we must eternally sing His praise and do His will. Let us dance to the tune of His *bansi* — flute, and all would be well.

17

Belief in God: One Yet Many[1]

A friend had asked Gandhi three questions in a most humble spirit. One of the questions related to Gandhi's belief in God. The question and Gandhi's reply are reproduced here:

Question: You have often said that God is an impersonal, absolute Being, free from passions or attributes, which means that He is not the author of the universe nor does He sit in judgment over man's virtue and vice. And you talk of the will of God every now and then.

How can a God without any attribute have a will, and how can you conform your will to His? Your *atman is* free to do whatever he likes. If he does not succeed in doing it, it is the result of his past doings, God has nothing to do with it. And yet *you* cannot be talking of the will of God to beguile the common folk, for you are a *satyagrahi.* Why then this fatalism?

[1] The Gujarati original of this appeared in *Navajivan,* Jan 17, 1926. This is a translation by Mahadev Desai.

Gandhi's reply: I talk of God exactly as I believe Him to be. Why should I beguile people into error and work my own perdition? I seek no reward from them.

I believe God to be creative as well as non-creative. This too is the result of my acceptance of the doctrine of the manyness of reality. From the platform of the Jains I prove the non-creative aspect of God, and from that of Ramannuja[2] the creative aspect. As a matter of fact, we are all thinking of the Unthinkable, describing the Indescribable, seeking to know the Unknown, and that is why our speech falters, is inadequate and even often contradictory. Then why do the Vedas describe *Brahman* as 'not this', 'not this'? But if He or It is not this, He or It is.

To me God is truth and love: God is ethics and morality; God is fearlessness. God is the source of light and life and yet He is above and beyond all these. God is conscience. He is even the atheism of the atheist.

If we exist if our parents and their parents have existed, then it is proper to believe in the Parent of the whole creation. If He is not, we are nowhere. And that is why all of us with one voice call *one* God differently as Paramatma, Ishwara, Siva, Vishnu, Rama, Allah, Khuda, Dada Hormuzda, Jehovah, God, and an infinite variety of names. He is *one* and yet many; He is smaller than an atom, and bigger than the Himalayas; He is contained even in a drop of the ocean, and yet not even the seven seas[3] can compass Him. Reason is powerless to know Him. He is beyond the reach or grasp of reason.

But I need not labour the point. Faith is essential in this matter. My logic can make and unmake innumerable

---

[2] A 12th century theologian; philosopher and scholar; also known as Sriramanujacharya.

[3] An idiomatic expression used for all the world's oceans and seas.

There is in Hinduism
room enough for Jesus,
as there is for
Mohammed,
Zoroaster and Moses.

hypotheses. An atheist might floor me in a debate. But my faith runs so very much faster than any reason that I can challenge the whole world and say, 'God is; was and ever shall be.'

But those who want to deny His existence are at liberty to do so. He is merciful, and compassionate. He is not an earthly king needing an army to make us accept His sway. He allows us freedom, and yet His compassion commands obedience to His will. But if anyone of us disdain to bow to His will, He says: 'So be it. My sun will shine no less for these, my clouds will rain no less for these. I need not force thee to accept my sway.' Of such a God let the ignorant dispute the existence. I am one of the millions of wise men who believe Him and am never tired of bowing to Him and singing His glory.

18

God: The Indefinable Power

There is an indefinable mysterious Power that pervades everything. I feel it, though I do not see it. It is this unseen Power which makes itself felt and yet defies all proof, because it is so unlike all that I perceive through my senses. It transcends the senses.

But it is impossible to reason out the existence of God to a limited extent. Even in ordinary affairs we know that people do not know who rules or why, and how he rules. And yet they know that there is a power that certainly rules.

In my tour last year in Mysore I met many poor villagers and I found upon inquiry that they did not know who ruled Mysore. They simply said some god ruled it. If the knowledge of these poor people was so limited about their rules I who am infinitely lesser than God, than they than their ruler, need not be surprised if I do not realize the presence of God the King of kings.

Nevertheless I do feel as the poor villages felt about Mysore that there is orderliness in the Universe, there is an unalterable

Law governing everything and every being that exists or lives. It is not a blind law; for no blind law can govern the conduct of living beings, and thanks to the marvelous researches of Sir J. C. Bose[1], it can now be proved that even matter is life.

That Law then which governs all life is God. Law and the Law-giver are one. I may not deny the Law or the Law-giver, because I know so little about It or Him. Even as my denial or ignorance of the existence of an earthly power will avail me nothing, so will not my denial of God and His Law liberate me from its operation; whereas humble and mute acceptance of divine authority makes life's journey easier even as the acceptance of earthly rule makes life under it easier.

> Since God pervades everything nothing belongs to you, not even your own body. God is the undisputed, unchallengeable Master of everything you possess.
>
> — *Ishopanishad*

I do dimly perceive that whilst everything around me is ever changing, ever dying, there is underlying all that change a living power that is changeless, that holds all together, that creates, dissolves and recreates. That informing power or spirit is God. And since nothing else I see merely through the senses can or will persist, He alone is.

And is this power benevolent or malevolent? I see it is purely benevolent. For I can see that in the midst of death life persists, in the midst of untruth truth persists, in the midst of darkness light persists. Hence I gather that God is life, truth, light. He is love. He is the supreme good.

But He is no God who merely satisfies the intellect, if He ever does. God to be God must rule the heart and transform

[1] Indian physicist, biologist who discovered and proved that plants also have life; Professor of Physics at Presidency College, Kolkata.

it. He must express Himself in every smallest act of His votary. This can only be done through a definite realization more real than the five senses can ever produce. Sense perceptions can be, often are, false and deceptive, however real they may appear to us. Where there is realization outside the senses it is infallible. It is proved not by extraneous evidence but in the transformed conduct and character of those who have felt the real presence of God within.

Such testimony is to be found in the experiences of an unbroken line of prophets and sages in all countries and climes. To reject his evidence is to deny myself.

This realization is preceded by an immovable faith. He who would in his own person test the fact of God's presence can do so by a living faith. And since faith itself cannot be proved by extraneous evidence, the safest course is to believe in the moral government of the world and therefore in the supremacy of the moral law, the law of truth and love. Exercise of faith will be the safest where there is a clear determination summarily to reject all that is contrary to truth and love.

I cannot account for the existence of evil by any rational method. To want to do so is to be coequal with God. I am therefore humble enough to recognize evil as such. And I call God long suffering and patient precisely because He permits evil in the world. I know that He has no evil. He is the author of it and yet untouched by it.

I know too that I shall never know God if I do not wrestle with and against evil at the cost of life itself. I am fortified in the belief by my own humble and limited experience. The purer I try to become, the nearer I feel to be to God. How much more should I be, when my faith is not a mere apology as it is today but has become as immovable as the Himalayas and as white and bright as the snows on their peaks? Meanwhile I invite (everyone) to pray with Newman[2] who sang from experience:

> Lead, kindly Light, amid the encircling gloom,
>   Lead Thou me on:
> The night is dark and I am far from home,
>   Lead Thou me on.
> Keep Thou my feet, I do not ask to see
>   The distant scene; one step enough for me.

[2] John Henry Newman (1801-1890) an English poet.

19

Advaitism and God

In answer to a friend's question, Gandhiji wrote.

I am an *advaitist* and yet I can support *dvaitism* (dualism). The world is changing every moment, and is therefore unreal, it has no permanent existence. But though it is constantly changing, it has a something about it which persists and it is therefore to that extent real. I have therefore no objection to calling it real and unreal, and thus being called an *anekantavadi* or a *syadvadi*. But my *syadvada* is not the *syadvada* of the learned, it is peculiarly my own. I cannot engage in a debate with them. It has been my experience that I am always true from my point of view, and am often wrong from the point of view of my honest critics. I know that we are both right from our respective points of view. And this knowledge saves me from attributing motives to my opponents or critics. The seven blind men who gave seven different descriptions of the elephant were all right from their respective points of view, and wrong from the point of view of one another, and right and wrong from the point of view of the man who knew the elephant. I very much like his doctrine of the manyness of reality. It is this doctrine that has taught me to judge a Mussulman from his own standpoint and a Christian from his. Formerly I used to resent the ignorance of my opponents. Today I can love them because I am gifted with the eye to see myself as others see me and vice versa. I want to take the whole world in the embrace of my love. My *anekantavada* is the result of the twin doctrine of *satya* and *ahimsa*.

I talk of God exactly as I believe Him to be. I believe Him to be creative as well as non-creative. This too is the result of my acceptance of the doctrine of the manyness of reality. From the platform of the Jains I prove the non-creative aspect of God, and from that of Ramanuja the creative aspect. As a matter of fact we are all thinking of the Unthinkable, describing the Indescribable, seeking to know the Unknown, and that is why our speech falters, is inadequate and even often contradictory. That is why the *Vedas* describe *Brahman* as 'not this,' 'not this'. But if He or It is not this, He or It is.

If we exist, if our parents and their parents have existed, then it is proper to believe in the Parent of the whole creation. If He is not, we are nowhere. And that is why all of us with one voice call one God differently as *Paramatma, Ishwara,* Shiva, Vishnu, Rama, Allah, *Khuda*, Dada Hormuzda, Jehova, God, and an infinite variety of names. He is one and yet many; He is smaller than an atom, and bigger than the Himalayas. He is contained even in a drop of the ocean, and yet not even the seven seas can compass Him. Reason is powerless to know Him. He is beyond the reach or grasp of reason. But I need not labour and point. Faith is essential in this matter. My logic can make and unmake innumerable hypotheses. An atheist might floor me in a debate. But my faith runs so very much faster than my reason that I can challenge the whole world and say, 'God is, was and ever shall be.'

But those who want to deny His existence are at liberty to do so. He is merciful and compassionate. He is not an earthly king needing an army to make us accept His sway. He allows us freedom, and yet His compassion commands obedience to His will. But if any one of us disdain to bow to His will, He says: 'So be it. My sun will shine no less for thee, my clouds will rain no less for thee. I need not force thee to accept my sway.' Of such a God let the ignorant dispute the existence. I am one of the millions of wise men who believe in Him and am never tired of bowing to Him and singing His glory.

20

Never Lose Faith in God[1]

Religious and moral instruction is nothing but character-building. So I say to the boys and girls: Never lose faith in God, and therefore, in yourselves and remember that if you allow refuge to a single evil thought, a single sinful thought, remember that you lack that faith. Untruthfulness, uncharitableness, violence, sensuality, all these things are strangers to that faith.

Remember that we have in this world no enemy greater than ourselves. The *Bhagavadgita* proclaims it in almost every verse. If I was to sum up the teaching of the Sermon on the Mount I find the same answer. My reading of the *Koran* has led me to the same conclusion. No one can harm us so much as we can ourselves. If you are, therefore, brave boys and brave girls you will fight desperately and valiantly against the whole brood of these thoughts. No sinful act was ever done in this world without the prompting of a sinful thought. You have to exercise strict vigilance over every thought welling up in your breast.

[1] Extract from a sermon of Gandhiji to students of a school in Trichur as summarized by Mahadev Desai.

Many students, both boys and girls, have often told me that whilst they understand with their intellect the force of my remarks, they find it impossible in practice to control their thoughts, and thus they give up the struggle and give way to despair, and then finding some evil books to stimulate themselves they nurse the evil thoughts. I want to draw a sharp distinction between the two processes that happen within us.

Except for perfect beings evil thoughts will arise in every breast. Hence it is necessary for us to offer incessant prayer to God to keep us free from evil thoughts. That is the process which does us good. The other process is to think evil thoughts and take delight in them. It is the most dangerous and harmful process and it is the process which I invite you to fight with all your might.

21

Equality of Religions

There is in Hinduism room enough for Jesus, as there is for Mohammed, Zoroaster and Moses. For me the different religions are beautiful flowers from the same garden, or they are branches of the same majestic tree. Therefore they are equally true, though being received and interpreted through human instruments equally imperfect.

'Warring creeds' is a blasphemous expression. And it fitly describes the state of things in India, the mother, as I believe her to be, of religion or religions. If she is truly the mother, the motherhood is on trial. Why should a Christian want to convert a Hindu to Christianity and vice versa? Why should he not be satisfied if the Hindu is a good or godly man?

If the morals of a man are a matter of no concern, the form of worship in a particular manner in a church, a mosque or a temple is an empty formula; it may even be a hindrance to individual or social growth, and insistence on a particular form or repetition of a credo may be potent cause of violent quarrels leading to bloodshed and ending in utter disbelief in religion, i.e. God Himself.

I have endeavoured to study the Bible with the eyes of a devout Christian and the Koran with the eyes of a devout Mussalman, and I have not hesitated to assimilate whatever I have found to be good in both these scriptures. I have studied other scriptures of the world also. But I have singled these out for the sake of illustration. But, you might well ask, if I declare all these religions to be equally true and equally demanding my respect, what is the meaning of my remaining a Hindu?

I shall tell you why. Latterly I have been endeavouring to describe to vast assemblages of men and women I have addressed what I regard as the essence of Hinduism, and I have been suggesting to them one incredibly simple mantra of the *Ishopanishad* and, as you know, it is one of the *Upanishads* that enjoy the sanctity of the Vedas.

> The very first verse of the *Ishopanishad* means simply this:
>
> God pervades everything that is to be found in this universe down to the tiniest atom. The mantra describes God as the Creator, the Ruler and the Lord. The seer to whom this mantra or verse was revealed was not satisfied with the magnificent statement that God was to be found everywhere. But he went further and said: 'Since God pervades everything nothing belongs to you, not even your own body. God is the undisputed, unchallengeable Master of everything you possess.'
>
> And to crown all, the seer says: 'Covet not anybody's riches.'

I suggest to you that the truth that is embedded in this very short mantra is calculated to satisfy the highest cravings of every human being — whether they have reference to this world or to the next.

I have in my search of the scriptures of the world found nothing to add to this mantra. Looking back upon all the little I have read of the scriptures — it is precious little I confess — I feel that everything good in all the scriptures is derived from this mantra.

If it is universal brotherhood — not only brotherhood of all human beings, but of all living beings — I find it in this mantra. If it is unshakable faith in the Lord and Master — and all the adjectives you can think of — I find it in this mantra. If it is the idea of complete surrender to God and of the faith that He will supply all that I need, then again I say I find it in this mantra. Since He pervades every fibre of my being and of all of you, I derive from it the doctrine of equality of all creatures on earth and it should satisfy the cravings of all philosophical communists.

This mantra tells me that I cannot hold as mine anything that belongs to God, and if my life and that of all who believe in this mantra has to be a life of perfect dedication, it follows that it will have to be a life of continual service of our fellow creatures.

This, I say, is my faith and should be the faith of all who call themselves Hindus. And I venture to suggest to my Christian and Mussalman friends that they will find nothing more in their scriptures if they will search them, and I want the aid of everybody on earth — whether he is a Christian or a Mussalman or what else — to help realize the lofty purpose that lies in this mantra.

I do not wish to hide from you the fact that I am not unaware of many superstitions that go under the name of Hinduism. I am most painfully conscious of all superstitions that are to be found masquerading as Hinduism and I have no hesitation to call a spade a spade.

Hinduism tells everyone
to worship God according
to his own faith or *dharma*,
and so it lives at peace with
all the religions.

I do not believe that these superstitions form part of Hinduism. The very canons of interpretation laid down by Hinduism teach me that whatever is inconsistent with the truth I have expounded to you and what is hidden in the mantra I have named, must be summarily rejected as not belonging to Hinduism.

22

The Traditions of Self Purification[1]

Though the majority of the Mussalmans of India and the Hindus belong to the same 'stock', the religious environment has made them different.

I believe and I have noticed too that thought transforms man's features as well as character. The Sikhs are the most recent illustration of the fact. The Mussalman, being heir to fresh traditions, exhibits the virility of a comparatively new system of life.

In my opinion, non-violence has a predominant place in the Koran, the thirteen hundred years of imperialistic expansion has made the Mussalmans fighters as a body. They are therefore aggressive. Bullying is the natural excrescence of an aggressive spirit. The Hindu has an ages old civilization. He is essentially non-violent. His civilization has passed through the experiences that the two recent ones are still passing through.

[1] Originally published under the title *What may Hindu do?* in *Young India.*

If Hinduism was ever imperialistic in the modern sense of the term, it has outlived its imperialism and has, either deliberately or as a matter of course, given it up. Predominance of the non-violent spirit has restricted the use of arms to a small minority which must always be subordinate to a civil power highly spiritual, learned and selfless.

The Hindus as a body are, therefore, not equipped for fighting. But not having retained their spiritual training, they have forgotten the use of an effective substitute for arms and, not knowing their use nor having an aptitude for them, they have become docile to the point of timidity or cowardice. This vice is, therefore, a natural excrescence of gentleness.

Holding this view, I do not think that the Hindu exclusiveness, bad as it undoubtedly is, has much to do with the Hindu timidity. Hence, also, my disbelief in *akhadas* as a means of self-defence. I prize them for physical culture but, for self-defence, I would restore the spiritual culture. The best and most lasting self-defence is self-purification.

I refuse to be lifted off my feet because of the scares that haunt us today. If Hindus would but believe in themselves and work in accordance with their traditions, they will have no reason to fear bullying. The moment they recommence the real spiritual training the Mussalman will respond. He cannot help it. If I can get together a band of young Hindus with faith in themselves and, therefore, faith in the Mussalmans, the band will become a shield for the weaker ones. They (the young Hindus) will teach how to die without killing.

I know no other way. When our ancestors saw affliction surrounding them, they went in for *tapasya* — purification. They realized the helplessness of the flesh and in their helplessness they prayed till they compelled the Maker to obey their call. 'Oh yes,' says my Hindu friend, 'but then God sent someone to wield arms.' I am not concerned with denying the truth of the retort.

All I say to the friend is that as a Hindu he may not ignore the cause and secure the result. It will be time to fight when we have done enough *tapasya.* Are we purified enough, I ask? Have we even done willing penance for the sin of untouchability, let alone the personal purity of individuals? Are our religious preceptors all that they should be? We are beating the air whilst we simply concentrate our attention upon picking holes in the Mussalman conduct.

23

Power of Ramanama

A correspondent had written a letter to Gandhiji mentioning his statement in a speech that he had thrice been saved from sin by *Ramanama*. Pointing out that a local paper, *Saurashtra,* had commented on this statement and drawn inferences which were not clear, he had asked Gandhiji himself to explain what he had meant. The original letter is not translated here.

I do not know the writer. The fact that he had the letter delivered to me through his brother when I was leaving Bombay shows the strength of his curiosity in this matter. My experiments are spiritual. Some of them are novel. They depend very much on self-examination on my part. I have carried them out, following the maxim: 'As in one's body, so in the universe'. The underlying assumption is that what is possible to me must be so to all others. Hence I have to answer some questions about private matters too.

Moreover, I cannot resist the opportunity I have got, in answering this question, of explaining the power of *Ramanama.*

I should, however, like to request this correspondent and others who may put questions to me in future that, if they base their questions on newspaper reports, they should send me copies of the papers in question. I have often stated that I do not read newspapers for the simple reason that I am not able to do so. I do not know what *Saurashtra* has written. It is difficult to take notes of my speeches. Mahadevbhai[1] does so, but I do not always, approve the notes he takes. The reason is that when subtle or new ideas are being expressed, an error in reporting even one word may misrepresent the speaker's meaning. Hence, when reporters who are not familiar with my ideas take notes of my speeches, they can never be relied upon, and I have often asked readers not to depend on such reports. When they have a doubt about anything, they may ask me and, while doing so, they should also send me a copy of the newspaper in which they have read reports of my speeches.

With these prefatory remarks, even though I do not know what *Saurashtra* has said on the matter, I shall describe how I was saved on those three occasions by the grace of God. All the three occasions concern public women. I was taken to two of them by friends on different occasions.

~

On the first occasion, I went to the place out of false regard for the friend and, if God had not saved me, I would certainly have fallen. This time the woman whose house I had entered herself threw me out with contempt. I simply did not know what to say or how to behave in such a situation. Prior to this incident I always regarded it as shameful even to sit near a public woman, so that I was trembling even when entering that house. After going in, I could not even look at her face and I do not know

[1] Freedom movement activist and Mahatma Gandhi's personal secretary.

what her face was like. What could that smart woman do to such a fool but turn him out? She said a few angry words to me and asked me to go away. At that time, of course, I did not realize that God had saved me. I left feeling miserable. I felt crest-fallen and even unhappy about my stupidity! I felt that I lacked manliness. It was later I realized that I had been shielded by my stupidity. God had saved me by making me behave like a fool. Else how could I, who had entered a house of ill-fame with evil intention, have been saved?

The second occasion was more dreadful than the first one. I was not so innocent then as I was at the time of the first incident, though I was of course more vigilant. Moreover, I had the protection of a vow administered to me by my revered mother[2]. But this time the place was in England. I was in the very flush of youth. Two of us friends were lodged in one house. We had gone there only for a few days[3]. The landlady was as good as a prostitute. Two or three of us sat down to play cards with her. In those days I used to play cards on occasions. In England a mother and a son can, and do, play cards for innocent amusement. On this occasion too, we sat down to play following the usual custom. The beginning was completely innocent. I, of course, did not know that the landlady lived on her body. But as the play warmed up, the atmosphere changed. The woman started making gestures. I was observing my friend. He had abandoned all restraints. I felt tempted. I was flushed in the face, for lust had entered me and I had become impatient.

But who can harm him whom Rama protects? To be sure, His name was not on my lips at that hour, but He ruled my heart. On my lips was the language of lust. My good friend

---

[2] Gandhiji's mother was unwilling to send him to England, but when he vowed not to touch meat, wine and woman, she gave her consent.

[3] In connection with the Vegetarian Conference at Portsmouth.

noticed my behaviour. We knew each other very well. He had seen me in difficult situations in which I had, with an effort of will, kept my purity. But he saw that on this occasion evil had entered my mind and that, if the night progressed while I was in that mood, I too would fall like him.

It was this friend who first made me realize that even immoral men have good instincts. He felt unhappy to see me in that plight. I was younger than him.

Rama came to my help through this person. He aimed arrows of love at me: 'Moniya!' (This is an affectionate form of 'Mohandas'. I remember that I used to be called by that name by my mother, my father and the eldest cousin in our family. The fourth person to call me so was this friend who, through his goodness, proved a brother to me.) 'Moniya, be careful. You know that I have fallen. But I shall not let you fall. Recall the promise you have made to your mother. This thing is not for you. Be off from here. Go to bed. Are you gone? Throw off the cards.'

I do not remember whether I replied to him. I put down the cards. For a moment I felt unhappy. I felt ashamed and my heart began to beat fast. I got up and went to bed.

I woke up. I started repeating the name of Rama. 'How miraculously I have been saved, how He has saved me! All honour to my promise! All glory to my mother! All glory to my friend! All glory to Rama!' — I kept saying to myself. For me this was indeed a miracle. If my friend had not shot at me the invincible arrows of Rama, where would I have been today?

He on whom Rama's arrows have lighted — he knows what they are. He on whom love's arrows have lighted — he knows what they are. For me, this was an occasion when I first became aware of the existence of God.

~

If today the whole of world told me that there is no God, no Rama, I would say it lied. If I had fallen on that terrible night, I would not today be waging battles of *satyagraha,* would not be washing away the filth of untouchability, would not be repeating the holy name of the spinning-wheel, would not regard myself fit to be blessed by the *darshan* of millions of women, and would not be surrounded by hundreds of thousands of them who sit near me without fear as they sit around *a* child. I would always be running away from them, and they would have quite justifiably kept themselves at a distance from me. I look upon this occasion as the most perilous in my life. Seeking pleasure I learnt self-restraint. On the path to forsake Rama's name, I had his *darshan.* A miracle indeed.

Oh scion of Raghu's race, protect my honour, I am a fallen man, old in my evil ways; Take my boat safely to the other shore.

~

The third incident is amusing. During one of my journeys, I came into fairly close contact with the ship's captain, as also with an English passenger. In every port where the ship weighted anchor, the captain and some passengers would go and search for brothels. The captain once invited me to go with him and see the port. I did not know what that meant. We went and stood before a prostitute's house. Then I knew what was meant by going to see a port. Three women were produced before us. I was completely taken aback, but felt too embarrassed to say anything. Nor could I run away. I had of course no wish to indulge in this immoral pleasure. Those two went into the rooms. The third woman led me into her own room. While I was still thinking what I should do, the other two came out of the rooms. I do not know what that woman must have thought about me. She stood smiling before me, but that did not have the slightest effect on me. Since we spoke different languages, there was no question of my talking to her. Those friends shouted for me and so I went out. I certainly felt a little humiliated. They had seen that I was a fool in these matters. They even joked between themselves on this point. They pitied me, of course. From that day, I was enrolled among the fools of the world, as far as the captain was concerned. He never invited me again to see a port. If I had remained in the room longer or if I had known that woman's language, I do not know what would have been my plight. But I certainly realized that day, too, I was not saved by my own power, but that it was God who had protected me by having made me stupid in such matters.

~

I remembered only these three incidents at the time of the speech in question. The reader should not think that I have not been through more of similar experiences. But I certainly wish

---

I must repeat for the thousandth time that *Ramanama* is one of the many names for God. The same prayer meetings have recitations from the Koran and the Zend Avesta. Devout Muslims, for the very reason that they are devout, have never objected to the chant of *Ramanama*. *Ramanama* is not an idle chant. It is conceived as a mode of addressing the all-pervasive God known to me, as to millions of Hindus, by the familiar name of *Ramanama*. *'Nama'* at the end of Rama is the most significant part. It means the *'nama'* without the Rama of history.

Sevagram, Aug 8, 1946, Harijan, Aug 18, 1946

---

to state that every time I escaped, thanks to *Ramanama.* God gives the strength only to weak who approach Him in utter helplessness.

So long as the elephant trusted to his own strength,
So long his efforts availed him not.
Let the weak appeal to Rama's strength,
He will come to help
Before the name is uttered in full.

~

What, then, does this *Ramanama* mean? Is it something to be repeated parrot-like? Certainly not. If that were so, all of us would win deliverance by repeating it mechanically. *Ramanama* ought to be repeated from the depth of one's heart; it would not then matter if the words are not pronounced correctly. The broken words which proceed from the heart are acceptable in God's court. Even though the heart cries out 'Mara, mara'[4], this appeal of the heart will be recorded in one's credit column. On the contrary, though the tongue may pronounce the name of Rama correctly, if the lord of that heart is Ravana, the correct repetition of Rama's name will be recorded in one's debit column.

Tulsidas did not sing the glory of *Ramanama* for the benefit of the hypocrite who 'has Rama's name on his lips and a knife under his arm.' His wise calculations will go wrong, while the seeming errors of the man who has installed Rama in his heart will succeed. Rama alone can repair one's fortunes and so the poet Surdas[5], lover of God, sings:

---

4 Rama pronounced wrongly, that is, in the reverse, and then meaning 'dying,dying'.

5 A medieval hindi poet.

He is a Hindu who believes
in God, immortality of the soul,
transmigration, the law of *karma*
and *moksha,* and who tries to
practice truth and *ahimsa*
in daily life and understands
and tries to act according
to the law of *Varnashrama.*

Who will repair my fortunes?
  O who else but Rama?
Everyone is a friend of his
  On whom good fortune smiles,
None of his whom fortune has forsaken.

The reader, therefore, should understand clearly that *Ramanama* is a matter of the heart. Where speech and the mind are not in harmony with each other, mere speech is falsehood, no more than pretense or play words. Such chanting may well deceive the world, but can Rama who dwells in man's heart be deceived?

Hanuman broke open the beads in the necklace which Sita gave him as a gift, wanting to see whether they were inscribed with Rama's name. Some courtiers who thought themselves wise asked him why he showed disrespect to Sita's necklace. Hanuman's reply was that, if the beads were not inscribed with Rama's name inside, then every necklace given to him by Sita was a burden to him. The wise courtiers thereupon smilingly asked him if Rama's name was inscribed in his heart. Hanuman drew out his knife and, cutting open his chest said: 'Now look inside. Tell me if you see anything else there except Rama's name.' The courtiers felt ashamed. Flowers rained on Hanuman from the sky, and from that day Hanuman's name is always invoked when Rama's story is recited.

This may be only a legend or a dramatist's invention. Its moral is valid for all time: only that which is in one's heart is true.

24

Ramanama: One of the Many Names of God[1]

Ramanama is not for the few; it is for all. He who takes His name lays by a rich store for himself, and it is inexhautible. The more you draw upon it, the more it increases. It is infinite.

As the *Upanishad* says, you take infinite out of infinite and infinite remains behind[2]. It is the unfailing panacea for all the ills, physical, mental and spiritual to which man is subject.

Rama is only one of the numerous names of God. In fact there are as many names of God as there are human beings in the world. You may substitute Krishna for Rama or you can substitute for it any of His countless names and it will make no difference.

---

1 In a speech at Prayer Meeting, Mussoorie, June 2, 1946.

2 The invocatory *mantra* in *Svetasvataropanisad* reads:

That (the *Brahman*) is whole.
This (the Universe) is whole.
From the Whole has come out the Whole.
When whole is taken away from the Whole.
What is left is Whole.

I used to be frightened of ghosts and evil spirits in the dark. My nurse told me, 'If you repeat *Ramanama* all the ghosts and evil spirits will vanish.' I accepted her advice with all the unquestioning faith of a child. That cured me of my cowardice. (If that was the experience of a child, how much more would the grown-ups stand to gain by it if they repeated *Ramanama* with understanding and faith, he asked.)

Do evil thoughts possess you, or are you tormented by lust or greed? Then there is no charm against it like *Ramanama*.

Supposing you are tempted to amass a big fortune by some easy and dishonest means. If you have faith in *Ramanama* you will say to yourself, 'Why should I amass for my wife and children riches which they might squander away? Why not leave them a legacy in the shape of sound character and sound education and training that will enable them to earn their living by honest industry and body labour?' Ceaseless repetition of *Ramanama* will dispel your delusion and false attachment and the living realization will dawn on you that you were a fool to hanker after millions for the sake of your dear ones instead of offering them the priceless treasure of His name which frees one from all bondage and wanderings. Filled with the joy of that realization such a person will tell his wife and children, 'I have not brought for you the treasure I had set out for but something infinitely richer.' 'Where is it, show it to us?' they will say incredulously.'It is the Name which is richer than all treasures' he will reply, 'because it quenches the thirst for all riches. It is enshrined in my heart.'

25

Significance of Dwija Ceremony

Do you know that from today you have become *dwijas*? What does the word *dwija* mean? It means twice-born. Today you have taken a new birth, so you have acquired knowledge today of which you were ignorant so far.

The shastri has told you that you are now worthy of studying the Vedas. That, of course, you will do, but the fuller meaning of 'studying of the Vedas' is a life in conformity with dharma. So far your life was devoid of the consciousness of dharma and *adharma* but now you have acquired that consciousness.

During a famine, the sage Vishwamitra stole meat out of hunger. Having done that, he had to perform many ceremonies before eating it. No meal can be taken without taking a bath and performing the *sandhya*. Hence he began these ceremonies. But, while in the middle of these activities, he realized how low he had fallen! He had committed theft merely to appease his stomach, and that too of meat.

He who was satisfied with fruit and vegetables and had reached the *vanaprastha* stage of his life had coveted meat!

These thoughts made him aware of his dharma. He took the piece of meat back to the butcher from whom he had stolen it and begged forgiveness. The latter was embarrassed at the sage seeking his forgiveness and said, 'King among sages, this shop is yours, satisfy your hunger as much as you wish.' This made a deep impression on the sage. He told the butcher that as from that day the latter was his guru.

There follows a long conversation between the two which is narrated in the *Mahabharata.* However, it is irrelevant for your purpose. I narrated this story to you so that you would get an idea of what religious life is like.

You have already taken a vow to keep your thoughts pure for twelve years and study while observing *brahmacharya,* but as from today you have begun thinking from the standpoint of dharma. You should not make the mistakes you have been making in the past as you have a new birth now.

And, before you do anything you shall ask yourself whether what you are doing is right or wrong. The sacred thread is useful from this standpoint. Otherwise, there is no need to believe that *dwija* means a *Brahmin.* A Brahmin is one who has awareness of Brahman. If, after receiving the sacred thread, we do not take a new birth, if we do not begin a life in accordance with dharma, it makes little difference whether we wear it or not. I do not ask anyone to wear the sacred thread, as it has become a mere outward ceremony. But those who wish to imbibe consciousness of dharma from the ceremony may well wear the sacred thread.

26

Tulsidas and Ramayana[1]

Several friends on various occasions have addresed to me criticisms regarding my attitude towards Tulsi *Ramayana*. The substance of their criticisms is as follows:

You have described the *Ramayana* as the best of books, but we have never been able to reconcile ourselves with your view. Do you not see how Tulsidas has disparaged womankind, defended Rama's unchivalrous ambuscade on Vali, praise Vibishan for betrayal of his country, and describes Rama as an avatar in spite of his gross injustice to Sita?

What beauty do you find in a book like this? Would the poetic beauty of the book compensate for everything else? If it is so, then we venture to suggest that you have no qualifications for the task.

I admit that if we take the criticisms of every point individually they will be found difficult to refute and the whole

---

[1] The Hindi original of this appeared in *Hindi Navajivan*, Oct 10, 1929. This is a translation by Pyarelal which appeared in *Young India*, Oct 31, 1929.

of the *Ramayana* can, in this manner, be easily condemned. But that can be said of almost everything and everybody.

There is a story related about a celebrated artist that in order to answer his critics he put his picture in a show window and invited visitors to indicate their opinion by marking the spot they did not like. The result was that there was hardly any portion that was not covered by the critics' marks. As a matter of fact, however, the picture was a masterpiece of art.

Indeed even the Vedas, the Bible and the Koran have not been exempt from condemnation. But their lovers fail to discover those faults in them. In order to arrive at a proper estimate of a book it must be judged as a whole. So much for external criticism.

The internal test of a book consists in finding out what effect it has produced on the majority of its readers. Judged by either method, the position of the *Ramayana* as a book par excellence remains unassailable.

This however does not mean that is absolutely faultless. But it is claimed on behalf of the *Ramayana* that it has given peace to millions, has given faith to those who had it not, and is even today serving as a healing balm to thousands who are burnt by the fire of unbelief. Every page of it is overflowing with devotion. It is a veritable mine of spiritual experience.

It is true that the *Ramayana* is sometimes used by evil-minded persons to support their evil practices. But that is no proof of evil in the *Ramayana*. I admit that Tulsidas has, unintentionally as I think, done justice to womankind. In this, as in several other respects also, he has failed to rise above the prevailing notions of his age. In other words Tulsidas was not a reformer; he was only a prince among devotees. The faults of the *Ramayana* are less a reflection on Tulsidas than a relfection on the age in which he lived.

What should be the attitude of the reformer regarding the position of women or towards Tulsidas under such circumstances? Can he derive no help whatever from Tulsidas? The reply is emphatically 'he can'. In spite of disparaging remarks about women in the *Ramayana* it should not be forgotten that in it Tulsidas has presented to the world his matchless picture of Sita. Where would be Rama without Sita? We find a host of other ennobling figures like Kausalya, Sumitra, etc, in the *Ramayana.* We bow our head in reverence before the faith and devotion of Shabri and Ahalya. Ravana was a monster but Mandodari was a *sati.*

In my opinion these instances go to prove that Tulsidasji was no reviler of women by conviction. On the contrary, so far as his convictions went, he had only reverence for them. So much for Tulsidasji's attitude towards women.

In the matter of the killing of Vali, however, there is room for two opinions. In Vibhishana I can find no fault. Vibhishana offered *satyagraha* against his brother. His example teaches us that it is a travesty of patriotism to sympathize with or try to conceal the faults of one's rulers or country and to oppose them is the truest patriotism. By helping Rama, Vibhishana rendered the truest service to his country. The treatment of Sita by Rama does not denote heartlessness. It is a proof of a duel between kingly duty and a husband's love for wife.

To the skeptics who feel honest doubts in connection with the *Ramayana,* I would suggest that they should not accept anybody's interpretations mechanically. They should leave out such portions about which they feel doubtful. Nothing contrary to truth and ahimsa need be condoned. It would be sheer perversity to argue that because in our opinion Rama practised deception, we too may do likewise.

The proper thing to do would be to believe that Rama was incapable of practising deception. As the *Gita* says, 'There is nothing in the world that is entirely free from fault.' Let us, therefore, like the fabled swan who rejects the water and takes only the cream, learn to treasure only the good and reject the evil in everything. Nothing and no one is perfect but God.

27

Bhaktiyoga: Realisation of God through Devotion[1]

I run to my Mother *Gita* whenever I find myself in difficulties, and up to now she has never failed to comfort me. It is possible that those, who are getting comfort from the *Gita*, may get greater help, and see something altogether new, if they come to know the way in which I understand it from day to day.

This day I feel like giving a summary of the twelfth chapter. It is *Bhaktiyoga* — realization of God through devotion. At the time of marriage we ask the bridal couple to learn this chapter by heart and meditate upon it, as one of the five sacrifices to be performed. Without devotion, action and knowledge are cold and dry, and may even become shackles. So, with the heart full of love, let us approach this meditation on the *Gita*.

Arjuna asks of the Lord: 'Which is the better of the two, the devotee who worships the Manifest or the one who worships the Unmanifest?'

---

1 The two discourses sent by Gandhiji to members of his Ashram at Sabarmati, from Yeravda Jail.

The Lord says in reply, 'Those who meditate on the Manifest in full faith, and lose themselves in Me, those faithful ones are My devotees. But those who worship the Unmanifest, and who, in order to do so, restrain all their senses, look upon and serve all alike, regarding none as high or low, those also realize me.'

So it cannot be affirmed that one is superior to the other. But it may be counted as impossible for an embodied being fully to comprehend and adore the Unmanifest. The Unmanifest is attributeless, and is beyond the reach of human vision. Therefore all embodied beings, consciously or unconsciously, are devotees of the Manifest.

'So,' said the Lord, 'let thy mind be merged in My Universal Body, which has form. Offer thy all at His feet. But if thou canst not do this, practice the restraint of the passions of thy mind. By observing *yama* and *niyama* with the help of *pranayama, asana* and other practices, bring the mind under control. If thou canst not do thus, then perform all thy works with this in mind: that whatever work thou undertakest, that thou dost for My sake. Thus thy worldly infatuations and attachments will fade away, and gradually thou wilt become stainless and pure. The fountain of love will rise in thee. But if thou canst not do even this, then renounce the fruit of all thy actions; yearn no more after the fruits of thy work. Ever do that work which falls to thy lot. Man cannot be master over the fruits of his work. The fruit of work appears only after causes have combined to form it. Therefore be thou only the instrument. Do not regard as superior or inferior any of these four methods which I have shown unto thee. Whatever, in them, is suitable for thee, that make thou use of in thy practice of devotion.

'It seems that the path of hearing, meditating and comprehending, may be easier than the path of *yama, niyama, pranayama* and *asana*, to which I have referred; easier than that may be concentration and worship; and again easier than concentration may be renunciation of the fruits of works. The same method cannot be equally easy for every one; some may have to turn for help to all these methods. They are certainly intermixed. In any case thou wishest to be a devotee. Achieve that goal by whatever method thou canst. My part is simply to tell thee whom to count a true devotee. A devotee hates no one; bears no grudge against any one; befriends all creatures; is merciful to all.

To accomplish this he eliminates all personal attachments; his ego is dissolved and he becomes as nothing; for him grief and happiness are one; he forgives those who trespass against himself, as he hungers for forgiveness from the world for his own faults; he dwells in contentment; he is firm in his good resolves; he surrenders to Me his mind, his intellect, his all. He never causes in other beings trouble or fear, himself knowing no trouble or fear through others. My devotee is free from joy and sorrow, pleasure and pain. He has no desires, he is pure, skilful and wise. He has renounced all ambitious undertakings. He stands by his resolves, renouncing their good or bad fruit; he remains unconcerned. Such a one knows not enemies or friends, is beyond honour or disgrace.

'In peace and silence, contented with whatever may come his way, he lives inwardly as if alone, and always remains calm no matter what may be going on around him. One who lives in this manner, full of faith, he is My "beloved devotee".'

28

Anasaktiyoga: Gospel of Selfless Action[1]

It has been my endeavour, as also that of some companions, to reduce to practice the teaching of the *Gita* as I have understood it. The *Gita* has become for us a spiritual reference book. I am aware that we ever fail to act in perfect accord with the teaching the failure is not due to want of effort, but is in spite of it. Even through the failures we seem to see rays of hope. The accompanying rendering contains the meaning of the *Gita's* message which this little band is trying to enforce in its daily conduct.

Now, the message of the *Gita.*

Even in 1888-89, when I first became acquainted with the *Gita,* I felt that it was not a historical work, but that, under the guise of physical warfare, it described the duel that perpetually went on in the hearts of mankind, and that physical warfare was brought in merely to make the description of the internal duel more alluring. This preliminary intuition became more

[1] This Introduction to *Bhagavad Gita* was first published in *Young India* in June 1931 under the title *Anasaktiyoga: The Gospel of Selfless Action.*

confirmed on a closer study of religion and the *Gita.* A study of the *Mahabbharata* gave it added confirmation. I do not regard the *Mahabbharata* as a historical work in the accepted sense. The *Adiparva* contains powerful evidence in support of my opinion. By ascribing to the chief actors superhuman or subhuman origins, the great Vyasa made short work the history of kings and their peoples. The persons therein described may be historical, but the author of the *Mahabbharata* has used them merely to drive home his religious theme.

The author of the *Mahabbharata* has not established the necessity of physical warfare; on the contrary he has proved its futility. He has made the victors shed tears of sorrow and repentance, and has left them nothing but a legacy of miseries.

In this great work (of *Mahabbharata*), the *Gita* is the crown. Its second chapter, instead of teaching the rules of physical warfare, tells us how a perfected man is to be known. In the characteristics of the perfected man of the *Gita,* I do not see any (charactertics) to correspond to physical warfare. Its whole design is inconsistent with the rules of conduct governing the relations between warring parties.

Krishna of the *Gita* is perfection and right knowledge personified; but the picture is imaginary. That does not mean that Krishna, the adored of his people, never lived. But perfection is imagined. The idea of a perfect incarnation is an after growth.

In Hinduism, incarnation is ascribed to one who has performed some extraordinary service of mankind. All embodied life is in reality an incarnation of God, but it is not usual to consider every living being an incarnation. Future generations pay this homage to one who, in his own generation, has been extraordinarily religious in his conduct. I can see nothing wrong in this procedure; it takes nothing from God's greatness, and there is no violence done to Truth. There is an Urdu saying which means, 'Adam is not God but he is a spark of the Divine.' And, therefore, he who is the most religiously behaved has most of the divine spark in him. It is in accordance with this train of thought that Krishna enjoys, in Hinduism, the status of the most perfect incarnation.

This belief in incarnation is a testimony of man's lofty spiritual ambition. Man is not at peace with himself till he has become like unto God. The endeavour to reach this state is the supreme, the only ambition worth having. And this is self-realization. This self-realization is the subject of the Gita, as it is of all scriptures. But its author surely did not write it to establish that doctrine. The object of the *Gita* appears to me to be that of showing the most excellent way to attain self-realization. That which is to be found, more or less clearly, spread out here and there in Hindu religious books, has been brought out in the clearest possible language in the *Gita* even at the risk of repetition.

The Bhagavad Gita is a big knowledge-feast; it is the very *amrita* of knowledge.

That matchless remedy (for self realisation) is renunciation of fruits of action.

This is the centre round which the *Gita* is woven. This renunciation is the central sun, round which devotion, knowledge and the rest revolve like planets. The body has been likened to a prison. There must be action where there is body. Not one embodied being is exempted from labour. And yet all religions proclaim that it is possible for man, by treating the body as the temple of God, to attain freedom. Every action is tainted, be it ever so trivial. How can the body be made the temple of God? In other words how can one be free from action, i.e. from the taint of sin? The *Gita* has answered the question in decisive language: 'By desireless action; by renouncing fruits of action; by dedicating all activities to God, i.e., by surrendering oneself to Him body and soul.'

But desirelessness or renunciation does not come for the mere talking about it. It is not attained by intellectual feat. It is attainable only by a constant heart-churn. Right knowledge is necessary for attaining renunciation. Learned men possess a knowledge of a kind. They may recite the Vedas from memory, yet they may be steeped in self-indulgence. In order that knowledge may not run riot, the author of the *Gita* has insisted on devotion accompanying it and has given it the first place. Knowledge without devotion will be like a misfire. Therefore, says the *Gita,* 'Have devotion, and knowledge will follow.' This devotion is not mere lip worship, it is a wrestling with death. Hence, the *Gita's* assessment of the devotee's quality is similar to that of the sage.

Thus the devotion required by the *Gita* is no soft-hearted effusiveness. It certainly is not blind faith. The devotion of the *Gita* has the least to do with the externals. A devotee may use, if he likes, rosaries, forehead marks, make offerings, but these things are no test of his devotion. He is the devotee who is jealous of none, who is a fount of mercy, who is without egotism, who is selfless, who treats alike cold and heat, happiness and misery, who is ever forgiving, who is always contented, whose resolutions are firm, who has dedicated mind and soul to God, who causes no dread, who is not afraid of others, who is free from exultation, sorrow and fear, who is pure, who is versed in action and yet remains unaffected by it, who renounces all fruit, good or bad, who treats friend and foe alike, who is untouched by respect or disrespect, who is not puffed up by praise, who does not go under when people speak ill of him, who loves silence and solitude, who has a disciplined reason.

Such devotion is inconsistent with the existence at the same time of strong attachments.

We thus see that to be a real devotee is to realize oneself. Self-realization is not something apart. One rupee can purchase for us poison or nectar, but knowledge or devotion cannot buy us salvation or bondage. These are not media of exchange. They are themselves the thing we want. In other words, if the means and the end are not identical, they are almost so. The extreme of means is salvation. Salvation of the *Gita* is perfect peace.

But such knowledge and devotion, to be true, have to stand the test of renunciation of fruits of action. Mere knowledge of right and wrong will not make one fit for salvation. According to common notions, a mere learned man will pass as a pundit. He need not perform any service. He will regard as bondage even to lift a little *lota*. Where one test of knowledge is non-liability for service, there is no room for such mundane work as the lifting of a *lota*.

Or take *bhakti*. The popular notion of *bhakti* is soft-heartedness, telling beads and the like, and disdaining to do even a loving service, least the telling of beads etc. might be interrupted. This *bhakti*, therefore, leaves the rosary only for eating, drinking and the like, never for grinding corn or nursing patients.

But the *Gita* says, 'No one has attained his goal without action. Even men like Janaka attained salvation through action. If even I were lazily to cease working, the world would not perish. How much more necessary then for the people at large to engage in action?'

While on the one hand it is beyond dispute that all action binds, on the other hand it is equally true that all living beings have to do some work, whether they will or not. Here all activity, whether mental or physical is to be included in the term action. Then how is one to be free from the bondage of action, even though he may be acting? The manner in which the *Gita* has solved the problem is to my knowledge unique. The *Gita* says, 'Do your allotted work but renounce its fruit — be detached and work — have no desire for reward and work.'

This is the unmistakable teaching of the *Gita.* He who gives up action falls. He who gives up only the reward rises. But renunciation of fruit in no way means indifference to the result. In regard to every action one must know the result that is expected to follow, the means thereto, and the capacity for it. He, who, being thus equipped, is without desire for the result and is yet wholly engrossed in the due fulfillment of the task before him is said to have renounced the fruits of his action.

The Gita is not an aphoristic work; it is a great religious poem. The deeper you dive into it, the richer the meanings you get. With every age its words will carry new meaning.

Again let no one consider renunciation to mean want of fruit for the renouncer. The *Gita's* reading does not warrant such a meaning. Renunciation means absence of hankering after fruit. As a matter of fact, he who renounces reaps a thousandfold. The renunciation of the *Gita* is the acid test of faith. He who is ever brooding over result often loses nerve in the performance of his duty. He becomes impatient and then gives vent to anger and begins to do unworthy things; he jumps from action to action never remaining faithful to any. He who broods over results is like a man given to objects of senses; he is ever distracted, he says goodbye to all scruples, everything is right in his estimation and he therefore resorts to means fair and foul to attain his end.

From the bitter experiences of desire for fruit the author of the *Gita* discovered the path of renunciation of fruit and put it before the world in a most convincing manner. The common belief is that religion is always opposed to material good. 'One cannot act religiously in mercantile and such other matters. There is no place for religion in such pursuits; religion is only for attainment of salvation,' we hear many worldly-wise people say. In my opinion the author of the *Gita* has dispelled this delusion. He has drawn no line of demarcation between salvation and worldly pursuits. On the contrary he has shown that religion must rule even our worldly pursuits. I have felt that the *Gita* teaches us that what cannot be followed in day-to-day practice cannot be called religion. Thus, according to the *Gita,* all acts that are incapable of being performed without attachment are taboo. This golden rule saves mankind from many a pitfall. According to this interpretation murder, lying, dissoluteness and the like must be regarded as sinful and therefore taboo. Man's life then becomes simple, and from that simpleness springs peace.

Thinking along these lines, I have felt that in trying to enforce in one's life the central teaching of the *Gita,* one is bound to follow Truth and ahimsa. When there is no desire for fruit, there is no temptation for untruth or *himsa* (violence). Take any instance of untruth or violence, and it will be found that at its back was the desire to attain the cherished end. But it may be freely admitted that the *Gita* was not written to establish ahimsa. It was an accepted and primary duty even before the *Gita* age. The *Gita* had to deliver the message of renunciation of fruit. This is clearly brought out as early as the second chapter.

But if the *Gita* believed in *ahimsa* or it was included in desirelessness, why did the author take a warlike illustration? When the *Gita* was written, although people believed in ahimsa, wars were not only not taboo, but nobody observed the contradiction between them and *ahimsa.*

In assessing the implications of renunciation of fruit, we are not required to probe the mind of the author of the *Gita* as to his limitations of *ahimsa* and the like. Because a poet puts a particular truth before the world, it does not necessarily follow that he has known or worked out all its great consequences or that having done so, he is able always to express them fully. In this, perhaps, lies the greatness of the poem and the poet. A poet's meaning is limitless. Like man, the meaning of great writings suffers evolution. On examining the history of languages, we noticed that the meaning of important words has changed or expanded. This is true of the *Gita*. The author has himself extended the meanings of some of the current words. We are able to discover this even on superficial examination. It is possible that, in the age prior to that of the *Gita,* offering of animals as sacrifice was permissible. But there is not a trace of it in the sacrifice in the *Gita* sense. In the *Gita* continuous concentration on God is the king of sacrifices. The third chapter seems to show that sacrifice chiefly means body-labour for service. The third and fourth chapters read together will use other meanings for sacrifice, but never animal-sacrifice. Similarly has the meaning of the word sannyasa (has) undergone, in the *Gita,* a transformation. The sannyasa of the Gita will not tolerate complete cessation of all activity. The sannyasa of the *Gita* is all work and yet no work. Thus the author of the *Gita,* by extending meanings of words, has taught us to imitate him. Let it be granted, that according to the letter of the *Gita* it is possible to say that warfare is consistent with renunciation of fruit. But after forty years' unremitting endeavour fully to enforce the teaching of the *Gita* in my own life, I have in all humility felt that perfect renunciation is impossible without perfect observance of ahimsa in every shape and form.

The *Gita* is not an aphoristic work; it is a great religious poem. The deeper you dive into it, the richer the meanings you get. It being meant for the people at large, there is pleasing repetition. With every age the important words will carry new and expanding meanings. But its central teaching will never vary. The teacher is at liberty to extract from this treasure any meaning he likes so as to enable him to enforce in his life the central teaching.

Nor is the *Gita* a collection of do's and dont's. What is lawful for one may be unlawful for another. What may be permissible at one time, or in one place, may not be so at another time, and in another place. Desire for fruit is the only universal prohibition. Desirelessness is obligatory.

The *Gita* has sung the praises of Knowledge, but it is beyond the mere intellect; it is essentially addressed to the heart and capable of being understood by the heart. Therefore the *Gita* is not for those who have no faith. The author makes Krishna say: 'Do not entrust this treasure to him who is without sacrifice, without devotion, without the desire for this teaching and who denies Me. On the other hand, those who will give this precious treasure to My devotees will, by the fact of this service, assuredly reach me. And those who, being free from malice, will with faith absorb this teaching, shall, having attained freedom, live where people of true merit go after death'.

29

Are Shastras Infallible?[1]

'Should we not accept the *Parasharasmriti* as an infallible guide in kaliyuga?' he (the pandit) asked.

'No,' said Gandhiji, 'I accept no authority or no *Shastra* as an infallible guide.'

'But if you accept part of a *Smriti,* would you reject another part of it?'

'I reject the claim,' said Gandhiji, without softening his stern attitude, 'that we should accept the whole if we accept a part.'

'Then would you accept what is convenient and reject what is inconvenient?'

'That's a good question. Hinduism is not a codified religion. I shall give you what I conceive to be Hinduism. We have in Hinduism hundreds and thousands of books whose names we do not even know, which go under the short name of *Shastras.* Now when we want to find out whether a thing is good or bad, I do not go to a particular book, but I look to the sum total of

[1] Extracts from a conversation between a pandit and Gandhiji.

the effect of Hinduism. In Hinduism we have got an admirable foot-rule to measure every *Shastra* and every rule of conduct, and that is Truth. Whatever falls from Truth should be rejected, no matter wherever it comes from, and therefore the burden lies on the shoulders of that person who upholds a practice which is inconsistent with Truth, so that if a man wants to defend, for instance, untouchability, he has to show that it is consistent with Truth. Unless he shows that, all the authorities that he may cite in support of it are to me irrelevant.'

30

Manusmriti[1]

I hold *Manusmriti* as part of the *Shastras.* But that does not mean that I swear by every verse that is printed in the book described as *Manusmriti.* There are so many contradictions in the printed volume that, if you accept one part, you are bound to reject those parts that are wholly inconsistent with it. I hold *Manusmriti* as a religious book because of the lofty teachings contained in it.

Nobody is in possession of the original text. In fact, there is no evidence to prove that a rishi named Manu ever lived. Somehow or other, the genius of Hinduism has made the writers or the givers of the grandest truths efface themselves. Therefore I have suggested to seekers after truth the only safe rule for their guidance in studying Shastras, namely, that they should reject whatever is contrary to truth and ahimsa, the true foundations of all religions.

---

1 This passage is taken from an article which originally appeared under the title 'An Adi-Dravida's Difficulties'.

31

Significance of Shri Krishna's Life[1]

We do not know what Shri Krishna's life means for us, we do not read the *Gita*, we make no attempt to teach it to our children.

The *Gita* is such a transcendental book that men of every creed, age and clime may read it with respect, and find in it the principles of their respective religions. If we thought of Krishna on every Janmashtami day and read the *Gita* and resolved to follow its teachings, we should not be in our present sorry plight.

Shri Krishna served the people all his life; he was a real servant of the people. He could have led the hosts at Kurukshetra, but he preferred to be Arjuna's charioteer. His whole life was one unbroken *Gita* of karma. He refused proud Duryodhana's sweets and preferred humble Vidura's spinach. As a child he was a cowherd and we still know him by the name of Gopala. But we, his worshippers, have neglected the cow today.

1 The summary of the speech delivered by Gandhiji at Arsikere on Aug 20, 1927 in Mysore state. The meeting was held at the Travellers' Bungalow.

Hinduism abhors stagnation. Knowledge is limitless and so also the application of truth. Everyday we add to our knowledge.

Krishna knew no sleep or idleness. He kept sleepless vigil of the world, we, his posterity, have become indolent and forgotten the use of our hands.

In *Bhagavad Gita* Lord Krishna has shown the path of *bhakti* — which means the path of karma. Lokamanya Tilak[2] has shown that whether we desire to be *bhaktas*, or *jnanis*, karma is the only way, but that karma should not be for self but for others. Action for one's own self binds, action for the sake of others delivers from bondage.

What can be the altruistic action which can be universally done, by Hindus, Mussalmans, Christians, by men, women and children? I have tried to demonstrate that spinning alone is that sacrificial act, for that alone can make us do something in God's name, something for the poorest, something that can infuse activity in their idle limbs.

Lord Krishna has also taught that to be a true *bhakta* we should make no difference between a Brahmin and a scavenger. If that is true, there can be no place for untouchability in Hinduism. If you are still hugging that superstition, you can cleanse yourself by getting rid of it on this the sacred day of Krishna's birth.

He who swears by the *Gita* may know no distinction between Hindu and Mussalman for Lord Krishna has declared that he who adores God in a true spirit by whatsoever name adores Him. The path of *bhakti*, karma, love as expounded in the *Gita*, leaves no room for the despising of man by man.

---

[2] Possible reference to Tilak's *Gita Rahasya.*

32

How to Celebrate Diwali?

It would be no exaggeration to say that in this kaliyuga we have no right to celebrate Diwali with so much jubilation. Our celebrating Diwali implies that we feel we are living in Ramarajya[1]. Do we have *Ramarajya* in India today?

A king who is not prepared to listen to his subjects, under whose rule the subjects get no milk to drink, no food to eat and no cloth to wear, a king who massacres his innocent subjects, who trades in wine, hemp and opium, who, by eating pork, hurts the feelings of Muslims and by eating beef the feelings of Hindu, who threatens the very existence of Islam and gambles at horse-racing — how can the subjects of such a king celebrate Diwali?

I am convinced that never under Moghul rule, or at any other time, were the people so thoroughly emasculated as they are today. This is no accidental result but has been deliberately brought about, and so I look upon this rule as *Ramarajya*. The

[1] In Gandhiji's own words, 'The ideal of *Ramrajya* is undoubtedly one of true democracy in which the meanest citizen could be sure of swift justice without elaborate or costly procedure... I do not mean dhuali Raj. I mean the Divine Raj.'

government we dream of, I describe as *Ramarajya. Swaraj* alone can be such *Ramarajya.*

How may we establish it?

In former times, the subjects did *tapascharya* when they were oppressed. They believed that it was because of their sins that they got a wicked king and so they tried to purify themselves. The first step in this was to recognize a monster as such and avoid him, to non-cooperate with him. Even non-cooperation requires courage. To cultivate it, one needs to give up comforts and pleasures. To receive education provided by wicked Government, to accept honours at its hands, to seek settlement of one's disputes through its agency, to help it in framing laws, to provide it with policemen, to wear cloth produced by it, to do this while desiring that it should perish is like trying to cut off the branch on which one is sitting.

This, at any rate, we should not do during Diwali:

1. Treat ourselves to pleasures, Gamble,
2. Prepare all manner of sweet dishes, and
3. Enjoy ourselves with fire-works.

True Diwali[2] will come when *swaraj* is won. Let us remember that Diwali represents the annual celebration of the victory of the forces of Rama — that is, non-violence and truth — over those of Ravana — violence and untruth.

London, Nov 9, 1931
Bombay Chronicle, Nov 10, 1931

---

[2] It being his Silence-day, Gandhiji wrote this message on a slip of paper when a correspondent wished him a Happy Diwali.

The money saved by renouncing these things, we should donate for (true) *swaraj* work.

This is the duty dictated by these difficult times. When we have the Government of our dream, we may enjoy some innocent pleasures. At present, however, the people are in mourning, they are widowed. At such a time, they can have no celebrations.

33

Who is a True Vaishnava?

A true *Vaishnava* is he —
    Who is moved by others' sufferings;
Who helps people in distress,
    And feels no pride for having done so.
Respectful to everyone in the world,
    He speaks ill of none;
Is self-controlled in action, speech and thought —
    Twice-blessed the mother who bore such a one.
He has an equal-seeing eye, and is free from all craving.
    Another's wife is to him a mother;
His tongue utters no untruth,
    And never his hand touches another's wealth;
Moha and *maya* have no power over him,
    In his mind reigns abiding detachment;
He dances with rapture to Rama's name —
    No centre of pilgrimage but is present in his person.
A man he is without greed and cunning,
    And purged of anger and desire;

Offering reverence to such a one, says Narasainyo,
Will bring release to seventy-one generations of one's forbears[1].

~

From the marks of a *Vaishnava* described by Narasinh Mehta we see that he is a man who

1. is ever active in bringing relief to the distressed,
2. takes no pride in doing so,
3. is respectful to all,
4. speaks ill of none,
5. is self-controlled in speech,
6. in action and
7. in thought,
8. holds all in equal regard,
9. has renounced desires.
10. is loyal to one woman, his wife,
11. is ever truthful,
12. keeps the rule of non-stealing,
13. is beyond the reach of *maya,*
14. is, in consequence, free from all desire,
15. is ever absorbed in repeating Rama's name,
16. and, as a result, has been sanctified,
17. covets nothing,
18. is free from guile,

[1] This poem, which formed part of the daily prayers at the Ashram, appealed to Gandhiji as a perfect expression of his own ideal of life and seems to have had a powerful impact on him.

19. from the urge of desire, and
20. from anger.

Here Narasinh, the best among the *Vaishnava,* has given pride of place to non-violence. This means that a man who has no love in him is no *Vaishnava.* One who does not follow truth and has not acquired control over all his senses is not a *Vaishnava.*

He teaches us in his *prabhatiyan* that one does not become a *Vaishnava* simply by studying the Vedas, by following the rules of *varnashrama,* by wearing a string of basil seeds or the *tilak* mark. All these things can be the origin of sin. Even a hypocrite may wear a string of beads or put the *tilak* mark or study the Vedas or keep repeating Rama's name with his lips. But such a one cannot follow truth in his life, cannot, without giving up his hypocrisy, help people in distress or be self-controlled in speech, action and thought.

34

The Chief Value of Hinduism

An American professor in Comparative Theology on a visit to India to study Indian religions intelligently, asked Gandhiji to tell her in a nut-shell the chief value of Hinduism, as she had been told that 'Gandhiji was the life and soul of Hinduism'. 'It is hardly wise,' she said, 'to rest content to teach what you can out of books. One must meet the true representatives of these living religions.'

Replying to her Gandhiji said:

The chief value of Hinduism lies in holding the actual belief that all life (not only human beings, but *all* sentient beings) is one, i.e. all life coming from the one universal source, call it Allah, God or Parameshwara. There is in Hinduism a scripture called *Vishnusahasranama* which simply means 'one thousand names of God'. These one thousand names do not mean that God is limited to those names, but that He has as many names as you can possibly give Him. You may give Him as many names as you like, provided it is one God without a second, whose name you are invoking. That also means that He is nameless too.

The unity of *all* life is a peculiarity of Hinduism which confines salvation not to human beings alone but says that it is possible for all God's creatures. It may be that it is not possible, save through the human form, but that does not make man the lord of creation. It makes him the servant of God's creation.

Now when we talk of brotherhood of man, we stop there, and feel that all other life is there for man to exploit for his own purposes. But Hinduism excludes all exploitation. There is no limit whatsoever to the measure of sacrifice that one may make in order to realize this oneness with all life, but certainly the immensity of the ideal sets a limit to your wants. That you will see, is the antithesis of the position of the modern civilization which says: 'Increase your wants.' Those who hold that belief think that increase of wants means an increase of knowledge whereby you understand the Infinite better. On the contrary Hinduism rules out indulgence and multiplication of wants as these hamper one's growth to the ultimate identity with the Universal Self.

35

Hindu Code of Conduct

1. If we are not in the habit of waking up before dawn, we should form it.
2. There are many persons who start smoking immediately on waking up, others, little better, make the whole house aware of their having woken up by talking profanities. Instead of doing this, one should take the name of God before leaving the bed and thank Him for the night having passed safely.
3. On leaving the bed we should immediately awaken our children and then, sitting in a place which is not frequented by people, we should clean our teeth with *babul* or some other twig. We should use either salt or powdered charcoal which we must keep ready at home to clean our teeth and with the halves of the twig we should scrape the tongue and rinse the mouth well. We should sprinkle water over our eyes and remove mucus if there is any. Having done that we must wash our face, nose, ears, etc., carefully and wipe these with a clean cloth.
4. If one has to evacuate one's bowels and that particular village has no latrine, or if there is one, but one does not

like to use it, this function should be performed in a remote place which people do not frequent. The excreta should be properly covered with earth and the organs concerned should be properly cleansed with water. Thereafter the hands should be washed with water and earth, and the water-pot should also be cleaned well.

5. While performing this daily routine one should either hum *Ramdhun* or some devotional song. If one does not know any of these, one should merely keep repeating the name of Rama.
6. It would be daylight by the time one returns home. Other members of the family will also have performed their natural functions as mentioned above. All should then get together and sing *bhajans or kirtans* for five minutes to half an hour. So long as one does not know any such thing, one can at least repeat the name of Rama.
7. Thereafter, everyone should set out for work after taking breakfast. Children who do not work should go to school.
8. Before taking the midday meal, everyone should bathe with clean water and scrub the entire body. Dhoti, sari and such other garments should be washed. The poor who do not have the facility of daily change should wear a loin-cloth while bathing. The body should be rubbed and wiped after a bath.
9. In this manner, when night falls while performing one's daily tasks, God's name should be uttered after the evening meal and before going to bed and He should be thanked that the day passed without any mishaps.
10. The hands should be washed after every meal and after performing any task which soils the hands. After a meal, one should gargle and rinse one's mouth.

11. We should realize that God knows our every thought, sees everything we do. Hence no one can deceive Him. How then can we deceive out brothers and sisters who are His creatures? It may well be that these persons are unaware of our deception. If they come to know of the latter, how can we cheat them at all?
12. Hence we should sincerely serve those under whom we work and not deceive them.
13. And, if we do not deceive anyone, how can we commit any theft? Even cheating while weighing goods amounts to theft.
14. We certainly would not like anyone to abuse us or beat us or misbehave with our mother or sisters. Hence we should not abuse anyone, not even our wives and children.
15. Nor should we beat anyone. This includes our wives and children. These persons have to be separately mentioned because many men regard their wives and children as their property. But it is a grave error. In our religion the wife has been regarded the equal of the husband. Hence, she is known as the other half, co-partner in religion, a goddess. Children are not our property. Parents are the protectors of children. Hence, even with them, we should be gentle, tolerant and patient.
16. Just as we should have goodwill towards our wives and children, similarly we should treat our elders and our parents with respect.
17. And, as shown in 14 above, it is obvious that a man should treat another man's wife as his sister or mother and, similarly, a woman should regard another man as her father or brother.
18. Just as all men are creatures of God, so also animals are His creatures; hence they are also a part of the family. We

should therefore be good towards them too. We cannot misuse even mud or stones. Our religion teaches us even such prayer: 'Oh! Mother Earth, we walk upon you every day. We depend upon your support. Forgive us for touching you with our feet.' Having said this, we put a pinch of dust upon our heads.

19. And hence we should be kind towards our animals; we should feed them properly; we should certainly not overload them with burdens, we should keep them in clean places; and refrain from beating them.
20. Similarly, we should pluck leaves and cut trees only as much as we must. We should use discretion while doing so. We should not destroy wantonly.
21. So far as possible, we should avoid eating meat. Beef should be totally shunned. Cow-protection occupies a very prominent place in our religion.
22. In accordance with clause 19, all living creatures are our brothers and sisters. Hence, our *rishis* and *munis* taught us that we should regard the cow as our mother and should develop friendly relations towards all living beings including non-human creatures. It is in the fitness of things to regard the cow as our mother as she, like the mother, gives us milk. One who gets milk does not require fish or meat. Moreover, the cow provides us with bullocks and even after death gives us leather, manure, fat for carts, etc., and such other things. Hence, we should never kill a cow.
23. And if we may not kill a cow, how can we eat her flesh after her death? No sensible people in the world eat carrion.
24. By becoming an addict, a man renders himself virtually insane; sometimes, he completely loses his senses. Hence

I believe that the essence
of Hinduism is truth
and non-violence.

liquor, toddy, bhang, *ganja*, opium and tobacco should be eschewed.

25. Gambling involves deception and the money obtained through it is tainted. Hence we should not gamble.
26. Others are as fond of their religion as we are of ours. Hence no ill will or have disputes with Muslims, Christians and followers of other faiths.
27. If religion teaches us that all are children of God, there can be no high or low among them and there should not be even the faintest trace of untouchability.
28. Finally, our religion also tells us that anyone who does not earn his living with the sweat of his brow, eats stolen food. Hence, everyone should earn his bread by engaging himself in such manual that each person should produce food grains, *khadi* and such other.

These things which I have often said on different occasions have been put down in written form here. Other clauses may be added to these when the occasion arises bearing in mind the universal elements like truth and non-violence, which are involved in them.

36

Is there Satan in Hinduism?

This article is reproduced verbatim from the Sept 25, 1925 issue of *Young India* in which Gandhiji publicly responded the doubts raised by him.

A few months back under a heading not quite justified by its contents you published a letter of mine concerning certain religious systems and the belief in God. Now I am tempted to put you a question concerning his adversary (according to Semitic beliefs), whose name you are so often using in your writings and speeches, not of course without effect, as witness the article 'Snares of Satan' in your issue of August 6, 1925. If it was only rhetorical effect that was intended thereby, because you were writing or speaking in the language of a people who have been taught to believe in Satan's existence through the Semitic creed of Christianity, then I would have nothing to say. But the article cited, among other things, does seem to point to a belief on your part in Satan's existence, a belief, in my humble opinion, quite unHindu.

Asked by Arjuna what was the cause of man's continual fall, Shri Krishna said: '*Kama esha, krodha esha*', etc. (It is lust, it is anger). According to Hindu belief, it would seem, the Tempter is no person outside of us, nor indeed is it one; for there are 'the six enemies' of man enumerated in the Shastras: *kama* or lust, *krodha* or anger, *lobha* or greed, *moha* or infatuation, *maya* or pride, and *matsara,* i.e., envy or jealousy. So it is clear, Hinduism has no place for Satan, the Fallen Angel, the Tempter, or as he has been called by a French writer (Anatole France), 'God's man-of-affairs'! How is it then that you who are a Hindu speak and write as if you believed in the real existence of the Old One?

This correspondent is well known to the readers of *Young India.* He is too wide awake not to know the sense in which I could use the word Satan. But I have observed in him a disposition to draw me out on many matters about which there is a likelihood of the slightest misunderstanding or about which a greater elucidation may be considered necessary.

In my opinion the beauty of Hinduism lies in its all-embracing inclusiveness. What the divine author of the Mahabharata said of his great creation is equally true of Hinduism. What of substance is contained in any other religion is always to be found in Hinduism. And what is not contained in it is insubstantial or unnecessary.

I do believe that there is room for Satan in Hinduism. The Biblical conception is neither new nor original. Satan is not a personality even in the Bible. Or he is as much a personality in the Bible as Ravana or the whole brood of the asuras is in Hinduism. I no more believe in a historical Ravana with ten heads and twenty arms than in a historical Satan. And even as Satan and his companions are fallen angels, so are Ravana and his companions fallen angels or call them gods, if you will. If it be a crime to clothe evil passions and ennobling thoughts in personalities, it is a crime for which perhaps Hinduism is the most responsible. For are not the six passions referred to by my correspondent, and nameless others, embodied in Hinduism? Who or what is Dhritarashtra and his hundred sons? To the end of time imagination, that is, poetry, will play a useful and necessary part in the human evolution. We shall continue to talk of passions as if they were persons. Do they not torment us as much as evil persons? Therefore, as in innumerable other things, in the matter under notice the letter killeth, the spirit giveth life.

Glossary

Ahimsa	Non-violence.
Ashram	A place of spiritual retirement; a hermitage; a place for study and disciplining life.
Atman	The Self; the Soul.
Avatar	An incarnation of God. This word usually indicates the ten incarnations of Vishnu, the God of preservation and sustenance.
Bhagavata	Literally meaning Divine-Eternal tales of Supreme God.
Bhagvadgita	(popularly known as *Gita*) a part of the great Hindu epic *Mahabharata* wherein Krishna is the divine hero.
Bhajan	Hymn.
Bhakti	Devotion.
Brahmacharaya	Continence; celibacy; self-control; also the first stage of a high caste Hindu's (usually referred to as *Dwija* in religious texts) religious life.
Brahman	The Ultimate Reality.
Brahmana	The first or the highest of the four castes sanctioned by the Hindu religion (literally, one who knows Brahman — Ultimate Reality); *see* Kshatriya, Vaishya and Shudra.

Darshan	Sight; vision.
Dharma	Religion; duty. A comprehensive Sanskrit term embracing the concepts of law, justice, duty and virtue rolled into one.
Dwadasha-mantra	*Om Namo Bhagavate Vasudevaya,* 'Salutation to Lord Vasudeva'; mantra or formula has twelve syllables; hence *dwadash.*
Dwija	A Sanskrit term meaning 'twice-born'; in the Hindu social system, members of the three upper *varnas,* or social classes — the Brahmanas (priests and teachers), Kshatriyas (warriors), and Vaishyas (merchants) — whose sacrament of initiation is regarded as a second or spiritual birth. The initiation ceremony (*upanayana*) invests the male caste members with a sacred thread, a loop worn next to the skin over the left shoulder and across the right hip. The lowest Hindu varna, the Shudras, and people whose status eludes the four varna system altogether are regarded as theoretically ineligible to study or even to listen to the Vedas, a collection of hymns in archaic Sanskrit.
Gayatri	Invocation of Sun-God, recited by the higher caste Hindus.
Guru	A preceptor; a teacher.
Harijan	Literally, a man of God; an untouchable. A term first used for untouchables by Gandhiji. Also refers to the weekly *Harijan* founded by Gandhiji in February 1933.
Ishwara	Creator, Supreme personal God.
Itihasas	Sanskrit for 'histories' — are supplementary Vedic literature which help explain the *Vedas* and *Vedanta Shastra.*
Kaliyuga	According to Hindu mythology there have been four Ages since the beginning of time, viz. *Satyayuga, Tretayuga, Dwaparyuga, Kaliyuga*, the present *yuga*, the Age of universal degeneracy.

Karma	Action; also popularly used in the sense of fate (accruing as a result of past actions).
Karmayogi	One who practices *karmayoga*, i.e., the doctrine of detachment in action.
Kshatriya	The second of the four castes (the warrior caste sanctioned by the Hindu religion); *see* Brahmana, Vaishya and Shudra.
Mahabharata	One of the great Hindu epics wherein Krishna is the divine hero.
Mahatma	Great Soul.
Mantra	A verse in a religious text; incantation.
Maya	Creation-illusion; veil hiding the Reality from man's ego.
Moha	Primal ignorance and the attachment resulting from it.
Moksha	Self-realization.
Nirvana	Nothingness; release from the cycle of rebirth; supreme bliss.
Pandit	Learned man.
Pinjrapole	Institution for tending cattle, particularly, old and infirm.
Prabhatiyan	Devotional songs with which the devout, getting up before dawn, commence the day.
Ramadhuna	Rhythmical chanting of the name of Rama — *Raghupati, Raghav, Rajaram*, etc.
Ramanama	The sacred name of Rama.
Ramarajya	Kingdom of Rama which was known for its beneficent and just rule; now used to mean any just rule working for the good of the people.
Ramayana	One of the great Hindu epics wherein Rama is the divine hero.
Sanatan	Believer in Hindu scriptures; also used popularly in the sense of an orthodox person.
Sandhya	Religious meditation and repetition of mantras accompanied by certain formularies like sipping water, etc.; a ritual practiced by higher caste Hindus at sunrise, noon and sunset.

Sannyasa	Renunciation of worldly life; the last stage of a higher-caste Hindu's religious life.
Sannyasi	One who has taken *sannyasa.*
Samskar	Essential and purificatory rites or ceremonies among Hindus like the naming of the child, first feeding of the child, thread-ceremony, etc.; conscious and unconscious, domestic, social, cultural and religious influences which go to the making of a person, mental characteristics.
Satyagraha	Literally, insistence on truth; clinging to truth; soul-force; truth-force.
Shastra	Hindu scriptures.
Shastris	Learned persons.
Shudra	The last of the four castes (the caste of labourers) sanctioned by the Hindu religion; *see* Brahmana, Kshatriya and Vaishya.
Smriti	The body of law as delivered originally by Manu and other law-givers to their respective pupils and committed by them, from memory, to writing.
Swaraj	Self-rule; self-government.
Tapasya	Penance.
Tilak	Caste mark used on forehead.
Upanishad	Sacred Sanskrit books of the earliest religious philosophy.
Vaishnava	One of the major branches of Hinduism.
Vaishya	The third of the four castes (caste of traders and agriculturists) sanctioned by the Hindu religion; *see* Brahmana, Kashatriya and Shudra.
Vanaprastha	The third spiritual stage in the varnashrama system. It lasts from 50 to 75 years of one's life and during this the person lives mainly in forest learning detachment from the material life and preparing himself to accept *sannyasa.*
Varna	Caste based on occupation; *see* Varnashrama. Also pigmentation of the skin.

Varnashrama	The system of four castes (based on occupations) and four stages of life (called Ashramas) for the first three castes (Brahmana, Kshatriya and Vaishya), namely, *Brahmacharya* (student's stage), *Grihastha* (house-holder's stage), *Vanaprastha* (forest-dweller's stage) *Sannyasa* (stage of recluse), sanctioned by the Hindu religion.
Yamas and Niyamas	*Yamas*, the cardinal virtues, according to *Yoga Shashtra* are: *ahimsa* (non violence), *satya* (truth) *asteya* (non-stealing) *brahmacharya* (celibacy), *aparigraha* (non-possession); and the *niyamas* or the casual virtues are, according to the same authority: *shaucha* (bodily purity) *santosha* (contentment), *tapa* (forbearance), *swadhayaya* (study of scriptures), *Iswarapranidhana* (resignation to the Will of God).
Yajna	Religious sacrifice.
Yoga	The science of control of the body and the mind; the science which teaches one how to unite, to join together, the individual self and the Supreme Self.
Yogi	One who practices Yoga.

Bibliography

Chap 1.
Young India, Oct 20, 1927 / *Collected Works of M K Gandhi,* Vol 40.

Chap 2.
Young India Oct 6, 1921 / *Collected Works of M K Gandhi,* Vol 24.

Chap 3.
Young India, Apr 8, 1926.

Chap 4.
Young India, Oct 14, 1926.

Chap 5.
Collected Works of M K Gandhi, Vol 4;
Collected Works of M K Gandhi, Vol 4.

Chap 6.
Indian Opinion, Apr 15, 1905 / *Collected Works of M K Gandhi,* Vol 4;
Collected Works of M K Gandhi, Vol 4;
Collected Works of M K Gandhi, Vol 4;
Collected Works of M K Gandhi, Vol 4.

Chap 7.
Young India, Aug 27, 1925 / Collected Works of M K Gandhi, Vol 32.

Chap 8.
Collected Works of M K Gandhi, Vol 22.

Chap 9.
Collected Works of M K Gandhi, Vol 22;

Collected Works of M K Gandhi, Vol 33.

Chap 10.
Young India, Nov 24, 1927.

Chap 11.
Translated from Gujarati. *Mahadevbhaini Diary,* Vol 1: Courtesy Narandas Gandhi.

Chap 12.
Yeravda Mandir, Chapter XIV-XV.

Chap 13.
Navjivan, Dec 10, 1924 / *Collected Works of M K Gandhi,* Vol 29.

Chap 14.
Navjivan, May 25, 1924 / *Collected Works of M K Gandhi,* Vol 28.

Chap 15.
Collected Works of M K Gandhi, Vol 54;
Collected Works of M K Gandhi, Vol 54.

Chap 16.
Young India, Mar 5, 1925.

Chap 17.
Collected Works of M K Gandhi, Vol 33.

Chap 18.
Young India, Oct 11, 1928.

Chap 19.
Young India, Jan 21, 1926.

Chap 20.
Young India, Oct 27, 1927.

Chap 21.
Harijan, Jan 30, 1937, *Collected Works of M K Gandhi,* Vol 70.

Chap 22.
Young India, Jun 19, 1924 / *Collected Works of M K Gandhi,* Vol 28.

Chap 23.
Speech at Prayer Meeting, Mussoorie, June 2, 1946.

Chap 24.
Navjivan, May17, 1925 / *Collected Works of M K Gandhi,* Vol 31;
Collected Works of M K Gandhi, Vol 91;
Collected Works of M K Gandhi, Vol 91.

Chap 25.
Harijan, Apr 25 1937, *Collected Works of M K Gandhi,* Apr 18, 1937, Vol 71.

Chap 26.
Collected Works of M K Gandhi, Vol 47.

Chap 27.
Young India, Nov 13, 1930.

Chap 28.
Young India, Jun 1931.

Chap 29.
Young India, Sept 9, 1927.

Chap 30.
Harijan, Apr 6, 1934.

Chap 31.
Young India, Sept 1, 1927 / *Collected Works of M K Gandhi,* Vol 39.

Chap 32.
Navjivan, Oct 31, 1920 / *Collected Works of M K Gandhi,* Vol 21;
London, Nov 9, 1931;
The Bombay Chronicle, Nov 10, 1931 / *Collected Works of M K Gandhi,* Vol 54.

Chap 33.
Navjivan, Dec 5, 1920 / *Collected Works of M K Gandhi,* Vol 22.

Chap 34.
Harijan, Dec 26, 1936.

Chap 35.
Harijan, Dec 27, 1936 / *Collected Works of M K Gandhi,* Vol 70.

Chap 36.
Young India, Sept 17, 1925 / *Collected Works of M K Gandhi,* Vol 32.

Personal Notes

Personal Notes

The Hindu world is like a sea. All refuse that finds its way into its bosom gets purified, settles down. There is no question of anybody embracing Hinduism. Everybody can practise Hinduism.